Nonprofit Issues and Management

Practical Help for Common Problems

<Harvesters Press>

<2017>

First Printing: 2017

ISBN-13:9781546449584

Harvesters Press
23 Sydney Ave.
Riverview, NB, Canada,

www.jefflutes.com

Dedication

To my mother.

Managing a household is the most important nonprofit organization there is and often the one most taken for granted.

Contents

About the Author

Dr. Jeff Lutes founded International Harvesters for Christ over twenty-five years ago. He travelled as an evangelist to small churches in farming and fishing communities in Atlantic Canada and today the work has spread to four continents. He would hold week long evangelistic meetings for these congregations. Today, there is a continual outreach with a network of eight radio transmitters in Halifax, the Annapolis Valley, Amherst, Charlottetown, Summerside, Moncton, Bouctouche and Sussex. There are several thousand listeners in the combined areas where approximately 700,000 people live. In addition to the radio work at home is the ministry overseas.

International Harvesters for Christ has a presence in over 30 countries. There are more than one hundred Associates with the majority in India. The ministry was founded in 1991, and see thousands of people accept Christ each year. One of the main purposes of the ministry is to hold training conferences for indigenous ministers in developing countries.

Biography:

 Born in Moncton, NB on October 22, 1962

Bachelor of Arts from Crandall University (1985)

Master of Divinity from Acadia Divinity College (1988)

Ordained Baptist Convention of the Atlantic Provinces (1989)

Founded International Harvesters for Christ Evangelistic Association Inc. (1991)

Doctor of Ministry from Acadia University (2011)

Jeff served nearly fifteen years as a pastor to the following congregations, Ripples Baptist (1981), Dorchester Baptist (1982-85), Cherryfield Baptist (1987-91), Shediac and Calhoun Baptist Churches (1993-1999).

He founded the following radio stations:

CITA FM 105.1 in Moncton, N.B. (2000), 99.1 Amherst, 107.3 Sussex, (2004), Bouctouche (2017)

CJLU FM 93.9 in Halifax, NS, (2005) Annapolis Valley 88.3 (2009)

CIOG FM 91.3 Summerside, 92.5 Summerside (2008)

This book is meant to help nonprofits overcome obstacles. It arises from more than twenty-five years of experience operating a nonprofit organization.

Introduction

Here are some key facts about charities in Canada from Imagine Canada: Charities in Canada

- Canada's charitable and nonprofit sector is the second largest in the world; the Netherlands is the largest; the United States is the fifth
- there are an estimated 170,000 nonprofits and charities in Canada
- half of these (54%) are run entirely by volunteers
- 2 million people are employed by these organizations representing 11.1% of the economically active population
- the sector represents $106 billion or 8.1% of the GDP (larger than the automotive or manufacturing industries)
- smaller provinces have a higher number of organizations relative to their populations
- the top 1% of organizations command 60% of all revenues

Developing a mission statement and a marketing strategy for the growth and development of a nonprofit organization are key to its success. Here are two fine examples. World Vision is an international partnership of Christians whose mission is to follow our Lord and Savior Jesus Christ in working with the poor and oppressed to promote human transformation, seek justice and bear witness to the good news of the Kingdom of God. The vision is "for every child, life in all its fullness; Our prayer for every heart, the will to make it so." The mission of the Boy Scouts of America is to prepare young people to make ethical and moral choices over their lifetimes by instilling in them the values of the Scout Oath and Law. This book will help nonprofits see the importance of developing a clear mission statement and how everything in that organization hinges on that precise, defining objective. Aspects of an effective mission statement will be examined. Next, we will begin to "brand" our nonprofit and then we will start to to market it. We will examine what it means to brand a nonprofit. Marketing is through various forms of media such as radio, TV, print and social media. We will discuss the amount of time and resources that should go into marketing and what should be the rate of return?

From there we will articulate ethical fundraising principles and methods of attracting and retaining new donors and sponsors. We will discover why is it so important that a nonprofit organization maintain ethical fundraising methods and examine the ramifications of failing to do so.

I intend to demonstrate differences and similarities between nonprofit and for-profit companies. A hospital may be a nonprofit but it certainly needs to have business like qualities in the sense that it demonstrates fiscal responsibilities. The balance between meeting human need and keeping within a budget are never more acute than in the operation of a hospital. Not all is negative when operating a nonprofit. For example, the manager of a nonprofit can accentuate the difference in the psyche of employees at a nonprofit organization as compared to those of a for profit organization. An emphasis can be placed on the non-tangible rewards of working at a nonprofit organization to keep morale high.

My plan is to delineate strategies to ensure long term viability of nonprofit organizations. Many nonprofits fail to stay in operation because they fail to operate with a similar structure and responsibility to a for-profit corporation. They place such an emphasis on the mission they fail to see the financial backing needed to carry out that mission. This leads to derision and eventually closure because common sense was not used in monetary decisions.

Unique challenges that face nonprofits can include but are not limited to a high demand for the service but a low amount of money to carry out the service. A business can simply lower prices and advertise more for example if it has a cash flow problem. This is not possible with most nonprofits because they do not operate in tangibles. How to rise above such difficulties creates unique challenges. For example, a Blood Services corporation or a school provide unique and vital services that carry with them a set of difficulties that are not going to be solved by following for-profit methods. There are serious ramifications for the public when there is a decrease in revenue for these kinds of services. It can affect the quality of service provided by health and educational institutions when the necessary funding is not supplied. The challenge comes for people in the nonprofit sector when the funding simply is not at hand.

We will recognize personnel problems and hardships that many nonprofits face and how to circumvent such difficulties. Nonprofit organizations are crucial for the well-being of society. It is important that universities, health organizations, etc. receive enough public funding or their effectiveness begins to decline. Heads of such organizations need to be effective in presenting these crucial services to receive the necessary monetary support they need to operate properly.

Those who head nonprofits need to exhibit a comprehensive knowledge of leadership and management skills necessary for directing a nonprofit organization. It requires an empathetic, yet structured person to manage a nonprofit. Firm but passionate again is another balance needed in the head of such an organization. An imbalance in either direction can lead to serious ramifications. These antinomies need to be kept in balance always to properly lead a nonprofit organization.

There is a growing dependence of governments on Non-Governmental Organizations to carry out relief and development. Fiscal cut backs mean nonprofit organizations are expected to do more with less. The government simply is not able to carry out the level of service it once did and this is greater a greater demand for nonprofit organizations to pick up the slack. Without a social safety net crime increase and the most vulnerable in society, children, the elderly and the sick are more prone to suffering.

It is important for governments to be at arm's length from universities, public health facilities, and other nonprofit organizations so they are free to offer nonbiased services. Universities need to receive adequate funding so they can carry out their objectives in an unfettered way. The poor need access to proper health care regardless of whether they can pay. It is inhumane to deny people health care because they cannot pay for it. This creates the dilemma of who is going to pay for it and how will the facility be managed. Regions of the country may be more prosperous than others yet the health needs remain the same. This creates unique challenges to ensure a standard of living that is equitable for all citizens.

This book will demonstrate how it is important for a nonprofit to have a marketing strategy for the growth and development. Some fundraising principles and methods of attracting and retaining new donors will be discussed. We will also look at a profile of what constitutes an effective nonprofit leader showing personality types, characteristics and management styles for problem solving methods, personnel issues, etc.

Chapter 1 Developing a Mission Statement

A mission statement is a foundational document for any organization. It is as important as charts are for the navigational officer on the ship to be able to reach the port. Typically, when an organization is registered with the government the mission statement is included in the incorporating documents. A company and its board of directors do well to refer to this often. It is the true North on a compass so to speak for a company. If a nonprofit organization wavers from its mission statement, the government needs to be informed. It is the Greenwich line for a company. It's the gold standard by which everything else is to be measured. Without a properly developed concise mission statement a nonprofit organization is a mishmash of ideas. When an organization has a clearly defined mission statement it has a higher likelihood of being effective and successful.

Nonprofit Issues and Management

This chapter will look at not only the importance of developing a mission statement but also the necessity of referring to it often. A marketing strategy for the growth and development of a nonprofit organization is often a natural outcome from a mission statement. The two go together and you can't have an effective marketing plan without a well-defined mission statement. It is the fuel in the tank so to speak to move the organization forward. It is not enough to simply have a strong mission statement. There must be a means of communicating the purpose and implementing the mission. Organizations with a clear sense of purpose are much more deliberate and effective because they do not waste time with peripheral issues. They can streamline their energies to achieve their desired objectives.

A mission statement is a central controlling idea. Everything the organization does must be tied to that theme. If an activity is not directly contributing to this essential purpose, then it must be jettisoned. All actions need to be looked at through the grid of how is this helping us to attain our objectives? If resources are being used for items that are not fulfilling the mission, then a stop spending order must be placed on all such purchases. If employee hours are being spent on non-impacting activities, then an account needs to be given to the director. This is particularly important for charitable organizations because then charitable receipts are being issued for matters that are outside of the mandate. There is a moral obligation to conduct all affairs in keeping with the mission statement.

A clear mission statement will help to ensure fiscal responsibility and the proper allocation of employee hours. It is helpful to post this mission statement where all employees and visitors to the office can see it often. It is wise to repeat this mission statement frequently during events in the life of the organization. It needs to be stated at the beginning of meetings, raised during staff discussions and memorized by everyone associated with the organization. It is a credo that is ingrained in the thinking of every person associated with the nonprofit organization. Everything that is done needs to be tied into this central theme. To do so will foster a team mentality and heighten productivity. Successful organizations have clearly stated objectives and a centralized mission.

A company that produces running shoes may want to develop as its credo, "Forming shoes to fit feet that spring to victory." This gives the sense that each running shoe uniquely forms to the shape of each athlete's foot causing a liftoff sensation with every stride. Every employee, down to the person who pushes a broom on the shop floor carries with him or her a deep sense of pride knowing they are helping to form running shoes that propel athletes to higher heights of accomplishment. If every employee knows the mission by heart, there will be a greater sense of productivity and quality. People no longer show up to work as mindless robots. They now have a deeper sense of loyalty, resulting in lower employee turnover. Lower employee turnover means greater long-term effectiveness. When people take pride in their work there is greater productivity.

Here are examples of mission statements or slogans that express purpose:

- Compassion Canada, "Releasing children from poverty in Jesus name."
- World Vision Canada - Sponsoring a Child Changes their Life and their community.
- McDonald's - I'm Lovin' It
- Coke - Share a Coke

Nonprofit Issues and Management

A clear mission statement is crucial to develop morale, give a sense of purpose and streamline the organization. A mission statement stated frequently generates enthusiasm and productivity among employees?

It is helpful to form your own personal mission statement. This will help you be the best person you can be at your place of employment. Answer these questions to develop your own personal mission statement:

- Ask yourself what you want to accomplish?
- If you had one year left and unlimited financial resources what would you like to see accomplished?
- If you knew that what you were about to attempt would not fail what would you try to accomplish?
- What things would you see as unnecessary and standing in the way of attaining your objectives?

Whatever comes to mind stop doing those things that are not helping you reach your personal objectives in life. When you have a clear sense of purpose and you can state it specifically then you have a mission statement. Anything that does not directly tie into the mission statement is superfluous. Divided loyalties and interests decrease our effectiveness.

It is helpful at this juncture to differentiate objectives from the mission statement. The mission statement is the overarching purpose of the organization. The objectives are tied into the mission statement and are to be subservient to it. No one objective is to overrule the mission statement. Objectives may have varying degrees of importance. They are not necessarily steps to accomplish the mission, rather, they form a composite to achieve the mission. The mission statement is the foundation for the house. The objectives are the walls and roof that represents the overall accomplishment.

Objectives and goals are somewhat tied together but are not interchangeable terms. They can both be long-term and short-term in nature. However, an objective is somewhat of a non-tangible while a goal is specific in nature. A child sponsoring agency may have a goal of obtaining 1000 sponsors in a month while an objective may be to provide educational facilities for the long-term betterment of the children. We see the difference between a goal and an objective in that goal is measurable whereas providing education is a statement of purpose. Goals and objectives all need to be tied into the mission statement.

A clearly defined mission statement, gives a strong sense of purpose combined with values that will be the driving force. The vision is the long term, overarching purpose. Objectives are what the company or organization hopes to accomplish. Goals are specific, and measurable.

A mission statement defines the reason for which the business exists; to provide strategic direction for the members within it. It is a statement of the overall purpose of the company and describes the attributes that distinguish it from others of its type.

How to Develop a Small Business Plan

by Daniel L. Garibaldi

When an organization has a clear mission statement, and objectives have been set out then it can begin to formulate a marketing strategy. A marketing strategy grows out of the mission statement. It is just that; a plan, and a formula to achieve the objectives of the organization. We spoke earlier about how a car needs fuel. It also needs wheels. When employees are enthused about a mission statement they are fueled to do the work, so to speak. They need to have a clear sense of direction.

Nonprofit Issues and Management

An organization or corporation needs to be well oiled in the sense that everyone does their part, and functions together. Without a marketing strategy, no one will know about the organization. Someone in marketing who is a professional helps an organization to objectify and delineate exactly what it wants to accomplish. It is the purpose of the person in marketing to help communicate this information to the public so that an action ensues. For example, it may be to have people donate to that organization. However, if the cause is not clearly presented to a certain segment of the population then no results will ensue. A good marketing plan puts wheels in motion for the organization.

A mass appeal is of some benefit. However, if the objectives and the mission statement are too broad few people if any will respond. Nebulous statements will have little impact. A clear statement of purpose on the part of the organization with a definite call to action will result in a certain segment of the population responding to the appeal. Vague statements will garner few results. A precise, clear call to action will bring about a change. It is important for the marketer to help the client identify their demographic they want to appeal to. Animal lovers may not be moved by pictures of children in poverty. Finding good homes for cats is not going to resonate with dog loves, for example. It is important to identify types of media that targets specific segments of the population and utilize these forms of communication to reach the donors that you are looking for. A vague statement of ideals will not resonate with most people. A clearly stated purpose for your organization communicated by an effective marketing strategy will yield specific results.

The mission statement articulates the dreams, goals, desired behaviors, culture and strategies of the business. it reminds people to focus on serving customers, for example. The mission statement, therefore, should be more than mere words on paper. It should be a living, breathing statement that provides both information and inspiration for everyone in the company so that they may work together in pursuit of common goals; therefore, it should be simple and direct not filled with jargon.

Although mission statements will vary greatly among firms, every mission statement should describe three primary objects of the company: 1.) its primary products, 2.) its primary target markets, and 3.) its overall strategy for ensuring long-term success. The mission statement is the starting point from which the overall business strategy will be developed. Like a cascading waterfall that has its origin some body of water, the topics covered by strategic plans all flow from and have links back to the mission statement. By way of example, the mission statement of Ben and Jerry's, the famous ice cream producer, follows: To make, distribute and sell the finest quality all natural ice cream and euphoric concoctions with a continued commitment to incorporating wholesome, natural ingredients and promoting business practices that respect the Earth and the Environment.

"The following are 50 mission statements selected from the top 100 nonprofits list (based on a series of web, social, and financial metrics). The best mission statements are clear, memorable, and concise. The average length for the full 50 organizations listed here is only 15.3 words (excluding brand references)

- ED (Technology, Entertainment, Design): Ideas Worth Spreading. (3 words)
- Smithsonian: The increase and diffusion of knowledge. (6 words)
- USO lifts the spirits of America's troops and their families. (9 words)
- Livestrong: To inspire and empower people affected by cancer. (8)
- Invisible Children: To bring a permanent end to LRA atrocities. (8)
- The Humane Society: Celebrating Animals, Confronting Cruelty. (4)
- Wounded Warrior Project: To honor and empower wounded warriors. (6)
- Oxfam: To create lasting solutions to poverty, hunger, and social injustice. (10)

- Best Friends Animal Society: A better world through kindness to animals. (7)
- CARE: To serve individuals and families in the poorest communities in the world. (12)
- The Nature Conservancy: To conserve the lands and waters on which all life depends. (11)
- JDRF: To find a cure for diabetes and its complications through the support of research. (14)
- Environmental Defense Fund: To preserve the natural systems on which all life depends. (10)
- Public Broadcasting System (PBS): To create content that educates, informs and inspires. (8)
- National Wildlife Federation: Inspiring Americans to protect wildlife for our children's future. (9)
- American Heart Association: To build healthier lives, free of cardiovascular diseases and stroke. (10)
- Heifer International: To work with communities to end hunger and poverty and care for the Earth. (14)
- ASPCA: To provide effective means for the prevention of cruelty to animals throughout the United States. (15)
- Kiva: We are a nonprofit organization with a mission to connect people through lending to alleviate poverty. (16)
- New York Public Library: To inspire lifelong learning, advance knowledge, and strengthen our communities. (10)
- Defenders of Wildlife is dedicated to the protection of all native animals and plants in their natural communities. (15)
- March of Dimes: We help moms have full-term pregnancies and research the problems that threaten the health of babies. (16)
- Monterey Bay Aquarium: The mission of the nonprofit Monterey Bay Aquarium is to inspire conservation of the oceans. (12)
- Amnesty International: To undertake research and action focused on preventing and ending grave abuses of these rights. (15)

- American Diabetes Association: To prevent and cure diabetes and to improve the lives of all people affected by diabetes. (16)
- charity: water: We're a nonprofit organization bringing clean, safe drinking water to people in developing countries. (14)
- Cleveland Clinic: To provide better care of the sick, investigation into their problems, and further education of those who serve. (18)
- In Touch Ministries: To lead people worldwide into a growing relationship with Jesus Christ and to strengthen the local church. (17)
- Human Rights Campaign is America's largest civil rights organization working to achieve lesbian, gay, bisexual and transgender equality. (15)
- Teach for America is growing the movement of leaders who work to ensure that kids growing up in poverty get an excellent education. (20)
- National Parks Conservation Association: to protect and enhance America's National Park System for present and future generations. (13)
- Save the Children: To inspire breakthroughs in the way the world treats children and to achieve immediate and lasting change in their lives. (20)
- The U.S. Fund for UNICEF fights for the survival and development of the world's most vulnerable children and protects their basic human rights. (18)
- Feeding America: To feed America's hungry through a nationwide network of member food banks and engage our country in the fight to end hunger. (22)
- Creative Commons develops, supports, and stewards legal and technical infrastructure that maximizes digital creativity, sharing, and innovation. (15)
- Make-A-Wish: We grant the wishes of children with life-threatening medical conditions to enrich the human experience with hope, strength and joy. (21)
- AARP: To enhance quality of life for all as we age. We lead positive social change and deliver value to

members through information, advocacy and service. (25)

- American Red Cross prevents and alleviates human suffering in the face of emergencies by mobilizing the power of volunteers and the generosity of donors. (21)
- Leukemia & Lymphoma Society: Cure leukemia, lymphoma, Hodgkin's disease and myeloma, and improve the quality of life of patients and their families. (18)
- Habitat for Humanity International: Seeking to put God's love into action, Habitat for Humanity brings people together to build homes, communities and hope. (16)
- National Multiple Sclerosis Society: We mobilize people and resources to drive research for a cure and to address the challenges of everyone affected by MS. (21)
- San Diego Zoo is a conservation, education, and recreation organization dedicated to the reproduction, protection, and exhibition of animals, plants, and their habitats. (20)
- Audubon: To conserve and restore natural ecosystems, focusing on birds, other wildlife, and their habitats for the benefit of humanity and the earth's biological diversity. (24)
- Boy Scouts of America: To prepare young people to make ethical and moral choices over their lifetimes by instilling in them the values of the Scout Oath and Law. (25)
- Mayo Clinic: To inspire hope and contribute to health and well-being by providing the best care to every patient through integrated clinical practice, education and research. (24)
- Susan G Komen for the Cure is fighting every minute of every day to finish what we started and achieve our vision of a world without breast cancer. (24)
- Ducks Unlimited conserves, restores, and manages wetlands and associated habitats for North America's

waterfowl. These habitats also benefit other wildlife and people. (20)

- Doctors without Borders (Médecins Sans Frontières) works in nearly 70 countries providing medical aid to those most in need regardless of their race, religion, or political affiliation. (21)
- NPR: To work in partnership with member stations to create a more informed public – one challenged and invigorated by a deeper understanding and appreciation of events, ideas and cultures. (28)
- The Rotary Foundation: To enable Rotarians to advance world understanding, goodwill, and peace through the improvement of health, the support of education, and the alleviation of poverty. (24)[1]

In *Transforming the Organization: A Social-technical Approach* Howard W. Oden, teaches an organization's mission statement, or its basic purpose, is its reason for being. It should set out what the organization is trying to become and show what differentiates it from similar organizations. The mission statement should provide a sense of significance to the members of an organization, regardless of their level. *"The most useful, vision statement focuses on markets rather than products,"* he says *"and should be achievable and specific."* He goes on to show that the customers or clients are critical in determining the mission of an organization. He also states, *"the mission should have an external rather than any internal focus."*

He further instructs that the mission statement should result in more effective performance. Goals should be measurable, realistic and achievable. A good manager will provide guidance for the future, but should not lead the organization into unrealistic ventures far beyond its competencies. Oden says, *"The mission statement must be sufficiently specific and detailed that it will be interpreted in the same manner by all who read it. Vaguely worded or ambiguous mission statements may do more harm than good."*

---

[1] http://topnonprofits.com/examples/nonprofit-mission-statements/

Nonprofit Issues and Management

An increasing number of profit and nonprofit organization across North America are incorporating strategic management activities into their overall operation. Strategic management can be defined as the *formulation, implementation, and evaluation of actions that will enable a firm to achieve its objectives.* The strategic management process is based on the belief that a firm should continually monitor key internal and external events and trends; a firm should seek to pursue strategies that capitalize on internal strengths, take advantage of external opportunities, improve internal weaknesses, and minimize the effect of external threats. Today the rate, magnitude, and complexity of changes that impact organizations are accelerating organizations. These changes are creating a different type of consumer, different types of products and services and consequently a need for different strategies. Increased competitiveness worldwide, coupled with rapid social, technological, and economic changes are major reasons why the strategic management process is being adopted by more and more firms.

A mission statement is a declaration of an organization's business or reason for being. A clear statement of the company's mission is essential to effectively establishing objectives, formulating strategies, setting goals, devising policies, allocating resources and motivating employees. I would like to reference, *A Framework for Developing an Effective Mission Statement* by Cochran, Daniel S.; David, Fred R.; Gibson, C. Kendrick in the Journal of Business Strategies, Vol. 25, No. 2 , Fall 2008 for further study on this subject.

> A mission statement is pivotal for good management. Employees of companies or organizations that clearly state their objectives and have a well worded mission statement feel empowered and focused. This increases productivity and employee retention.

Peter Drucker instructs in his classic book entitled, *Management: Tasks, Responsibilities, and Practices* a good mission statement is necessary for the formulation and implementation of strategies and makes evaluation much easier. The basic concepts on which businesses are built must be visible, clearly understood and explicitly expressed. He demonstrates that we cannot allow the organizations we manage to be at the mercy of events. We need to develop our values, policies, and what we believe in as companies and organizations.

If we do not clearly define what our mission and purpose is as a business or organization then we will be at the mercy of hostile forces that want to take over our market share, or worse still put us out of operation. We need clear, realistic business objectives. Drucker goes on to purport the, *"The business mission is the foundation for priorities, strategies, plans and work assignments."* It is the starting point for managerial jobs and structures. This Harvard sage states, *"Structure follows strategy."* The strategy will determine what are the key activities in any given business. Drucker purports that strategy requires knowing what our business is and what it should be.

Christopher Kenneth Bart is an accounting and budgeting instructor in Healthcare Finance. In 1993, Bart helped found the Management of Innovation & New Technology Research Center at McMaster University and was named its first director. The following year, he created the Innovation Management Network, a global association of professionals who collaborate through the Internet on matters of innovation and modern technology.

Mark C. Baetz is an expert in Strategic Management from Wilfred Laurier University. They conducted a strategic study. The introduction says,

> This paper examines the relationship between mission statements and firm performance using a sample of 136 large Canadian organizations. Previous writings suggest that mission statements are essential for superior organizational performance results. However, there is little

empirical evidence to support this claim. The data from the present study demonstrates that mission statements and some of their specific characteristics are selectively associated with higher levels of organizational performance. The paper concludes with several propositions to guide future research.[2]

Quoting from the executive summary of the same study in the Journal of Healthcare Management,

"At times, members of healthcare organizations may lose sight of what it is they are striving for. It is essential for both managers and employees in the healthcare industry to have strong organizational statements to turn to in times of change. Every employee can potentially influence the success of the organization in achieving its mission. External factors can make the healthcare work environment rather chaotic. An employee who has a clear understanding of the organization's purpose and values is more likely to make a decision that will lead the organization in the right direction."[3]

This journal made further reference to the same study by Barth and Baetz. It addressed the relationship between the mission statement and firm performance. The survey's sample population consisted of 136 executives from high-performing industrial corporations in Canada. They found organizational performance to be significantly and positively correlated with the degree to which an organization's performance evaluation system is aligned with its mission. The study concluded that

---

[2] The Relationship Between Mission Statements and Firm Performance: An Exploratory Study, Christopher Kenneth Barth and Mark C. Baetz, Journal of Management Studies, Volume 35, Issue 6, pages 823–853, November 1998

[3] Journal of Healthcare Management, American College of Healthcare Executives, July, 2000 Source, Volume: 45 Source Issue: 4

firms that develop mission statements with which they are satisfied, use a mission development process with which they are satisfied, and have high levels of internal stakeholder involvement in mission development, will experience the greatest benefits from their mission statements.

We can draw the following conclusions. When an organization or corporation organizes itself around a clearly stated mission, with, well communicated objectives that have been received by employees, and a reward system has been implemented to follow employee evaluations there will be improved performance. When employees, managers and all stakeholders align themselves with the clearly stated mission there is greater efficiency, than otherwise would be possible.

Chapter 2. Ethical Fund Raising Principles

Ethical fundraising principles and methods will attract and retain new donors and sponsors. This can apply to a charity that wants to attract new donors, a church that wants to retain members, a hospital that wants to maintain trust, or any number of other scenarios. I want to discuss image management because if you are following sound principles you will have will be perceived well.

Image Management

It takes a lifetime to develop a reputation. Sadly, however, it can be ruined overnight. We must guard how the public perceives us against those who would discredit us. We cannot fight everyone who has a differing opinion from us. However, we can and should in a practical sense correct those who would seek to undermine our intentions. Everyone is entitled to their own point of view. Some people are going to talk about us and there is not much we can do about it. Whether you are a proprietor, head of a mission, business owner, manager or operating a nonprofit, we all have this much in common; to one degree or another earning a living is contingent on having a good reputation. By and large, if we are following ethical principles we have little to worry about. It is paramount therefore that we maintain a good standing in public.

Let's begin by a brief discussion on the serious subjects of slander and libel. They are different but related matters. Both are criminal offenses to be punished by the law. Slander is purposely telling other people things that are not true. Libel typically refers to what is written or recorded. A charitable organization is reliant upon people's donations and cannot tolerate those who carelessly spread unfounded rumors. We need to be known for upright character and actions that are above reproach. If people lose trust in a nonprofit organization, it can have serious repercussions. One of the ways to fight this is to try to deal individually with disgruntled people and isolate the issue before it becomes contagious. While we cannot settle every dispute, we can try to see if there is something we can learn from the person who has a case against us. If it is deliberately malicious, motivated by jealousy or envy, then we must move quickly to quash it. Both written and verbal remarks that are unfounded need to be acted on quickly. Romans 12:18, " *If it is possible, as far as it depends on you, live at peace with everyone.*"

Social media can help increase the profile of a nonprofit organization. However, it needs to be monitored closely lest unfounded accusations are spread. If we are practicing ethical fundraising principles and methods, by and large, we should be relatively safe from unfair comments. If people, try to slander us most will recognize the accusations to be the unfiltered opinions of a disgruntled few. It is generally best for a charity to pay for an outside accounting firm to conduct an independent audit. This will help to silence critics. Counter posts on Facebook, or tweets can help set the record straight in terms of the honesty and integrity of an organization. Most fair-minded people will accept this.

Imagine Canada requires that each participant submit an updated financial statement and complete a short report outlining if anyone has launched a complaint related to the ethical code. Each year the person in charge needs to confirm that this code is still in use, and every two years the board needs to pass a resolution renewing their commitment to the code. If someone has a complaint against the charity they are encouraged to discuss their concerns directly, and that together the situation. an ethical code committee it should be established at arms length to deal with any unresolved issues. a certain protocol needs to be established in advance by the charity to attend to any complaints that may possibly be launched against it.

It is understood that not all complaints will be reasonable. While individuals are to be treated with respect, the motives of some complainants need to be examined to see whether their purposes are simply to create trouble. Most disputes can be resolved by allowing a donor to have full access to the audited annual financial statements.

Imagine Canada has the code that it expects all participants to follow. The first regulation is that all charitable gifts are to be acknowledged with a receipt. Secondly, all fundraising efforts by the charity will reveal its name and purpose that the funds are intended for next the charity when requested shall promptly make available its annual report with the business number assigned by CRA and if it makes investments what its policy is for investing money on behalf of the charity. The names of the Board of Directors need to be made available as well.in relation to planned gifts the charity will encourage potential donors to seek independent advice for estate planning, or anything that may significantly affect the donor's financial position.

If a donor requests to remain anonymous the charity must respect this wish. All donor records are to be maintained as confidential. Donors have the right to see that their own donation records are accurate. This code also requires of all participants that donors and prospective donors are to be treated with respect. That includes limiting the number of times that the donor is approached, and if the donor asks not to be phoned or reached by e-mail or to be removed from the mailing list. The charity must respect the wishes of the donor. If the donor lodges a complaint with the charity it must be promptly attended to.

In relation to fundraising practices solicitations must always be truthful and accurately describe the charity's activities and intended use of the funds. A charity that belongs to Imagine Canada is agreeing that it would never use marketing materials that misrepresent its objectives. The charity promises to never mislead or exploit donors. If it is using pictures or describing activities, they are always fair representations. When the charity is meeting with a potential donor face-to-face the solicitor will always provide verification of their affiliation with the charity. The charity promises always to keep safe and confidential, credit card numbers and any information about the donor. The charity shall not try to keep secret its fundraising costs and upon request, provide proper financial disclosure. The charity also agrees not to pay finders fees or commissions to third parties or employees who help to find donors. If the charity uses a third-party for marketing or fundraising it agrees to reveal how much is paid for the services.

The Board of Directors needs to be made aware if there are any problems arising throughout the year. All donations are used specifically for the charity's objectives as sated in its Constitution and founding documents. The charity is always to be concerned with cost effectiveness. No more than what is necessary is to be spent on administration and fundraising. All financial reports should be factual and accurate. (Source: Ethical Code Handbook: Imagine Canada)

With approximately 3,500 members residing in Canada, the Association of Fundraising Professionals AFP is dedicated to promoting and advancing the cause of its Canadian members. The Association of Fundraising Professionals is a document entitled Code of Ethical Principles and Standards for its members. It encourages transparency with donors. Ethical behavior will foster the financial growth of a charitable organization. Members of this organization would never knowingly do anything that would bring disrepute on the charity they represent. They would never engage in activities that would bring into question the organization. They are certain to avoid any potential conflicts of interest. They would never exploit their relationship with the donor or even a prospective donor. They comply with all local and federal laws. They present services honestly and without misrepresentation.

A member of this Association would never knowingly infringe on the intellectual property rights of another party. They protect the confidentiality of all information about the donors. They make sure that all materials and communications from the charity are accurate and correctly reflect what the organization is doing. They ensure that all contributions are used in accordance with the donor's intentions. They provide timely reports on the use and management of all funds that have been received. They adhere to the principle that all donor and information is the property of the organization and that if they share this information with another charity they give the donor, the right to have his or her name removed first. A member would not enter a contract to help raise funds, whereby an outside organization would be paid a percentage of the contributions that are raised and neither would pay finders fees. There is no performance bonus paid to people for raising extra money.

Those who are associated with a charity must conduct themselves with integrity, honesty, truthfulness and safeguard public trust. They are to inspire others through their own sense of dedication and high purpose. They must constantly be learning and improving their service for the charity they represent. They need to demonstrate concern for others and value privacy, and freedom for donors to choose which charity they will support. They need to be a credit to the fund-raising profession and encourage their colleagues to do the same. Anything that is contrary to the organization's mission and goals must be avoided. The charity must never exaggerate or convey false information to donors or falsify government reports. For example, if a board member owns a company he or she must not try to sway the charity to patronize them when it comes purchase time.

Ralph Waldo Emerson, is among several authors credited with writing these words, "Sow a thought and you reap an action; sow an act and you reap a habit; sow a habit and you reap a character; sow a character and you reap a destiny." Thoughts are like seeds our minds. Bad thoughts grow weeds and eventually crowd out what is good in our lives. Good thoughts, however, in time produce a good harvest. High ethical principles must characterize our every action. Our reputation is how we are known in public. Character is who we truly are. If we take careful steps to build good character eventually this is how most people will see us. Honesty is the best policy. The people that matter will come to trust us and that is what counts in the end.

Competitors may be able to undercut us. Someone said the sweet taste of a low price often leaves a sour taste in the end. If we practice ethical principles in time, they will be proven to be the way to build a lasting enterprise. Underhanded methods form a shaky structure that eventually comes crumbling in. Jesus spoke of building on the sandy riverbed and having our works washed away. We need to exercise the discipline and time to build on a rock-solid foundation. The organization is more likely to be able to stand the test of time when we have built solid relationships of trust with people. This may take longer but it is worth it in the end.

Even agencies with humble beginnings and modest incomes can be built to achieve significant revenues when sound ethical principles are enacted. The use principles include making the donor feel valued and respected. Take time to personally sign letters and send them out to donors. The added personal touch of saying thank you with a gift may seem trivial but eventually will result in increased revenue. A fruit basket is a wonderful way to show appreciation to a donor delivered directly to their home or office. Causing people to feel valued and respected are time honored principles for establishing a nonprofit organization.

The time it takes to write a thank you note is well worth it. A quick email to express appreciation is a wise practice. Remembering people's birthdays is worthwhile as well. Some charity workers have birthdays of donors recorded in their calendars so that each year they call that person to wish them a happy birthday. Another individual that I know visits people personally, calls them on a regular basis, and is often found taking guests out to restaurants to build strong relationships. Donor relations can be a tedious task, but a joyful one that is sure to yield a bountiful harvest. Gifts showing appreciation, so long as they are not exorbitant are justifiable expenditures. They let the person know that they are not just a number to the organization. It helps them to see that their gift is noticed.

Studies have shown that if a donor is receipted within two weeks of getting his or her donation they are more likely to give again. Some people don't like to see even a stamp wasted on sending a thank you note when they are monthly donors. The donor's wishes need to be respected, if that is the case. It is important to demonstrate that the charitable organization is being frugal with people's gifts. Those who operate nonprofit organizations need to respect the wishes of the donors if they do not wish to receive a thank you gift. A thank you gift does not have to be expensive to be meaningful. In fact, one should be cognizant that if the gift is of some monetary significance then it may need to be deducted for receipting purposes from the contribution. We do not need to get into trivialities but we do not need to remember that honesty, and accountability are always to be upheld when it comes to operating a nonprofit organization.

The Bible teaches that the worker is worthy of his hire. I do not think that because a person works for a charitable organization they should be paid less than what someone in a for-profit corporation is receiving. However, neither should they be paid an unreasonable amount because this certainly sends a bad message to donors. Accountability always needs to be shown to the donors. People who operate a charitable organization well should be compensated fairly. Salaries should be reflective of years of experience, education, and effectiveness. Nonprofit organizations that fail to pay properly will suffer the consequence of losing valued employees.

A long time ago I read a book that was extremely helpful. It is called, People Raising by William Dillon. Instead of fundraising, we should think of it as people raising in terms of building relationships with individuals. The premise of the book was that if we build strong relationships with people they are more likely to be steady donors. It is easier to retain a donor than to find anyone. It would be better to find out what discourages a donor than to always be trying to attract new ones. It takes many years to build a constituency. A nonprofit organization develops donations year after year when transparency and accountability are demonstrated.

Surveys are helpful tools to receive feedback. People need to know they will not be reprimanded for words of instruction they may have for the nonprofit organization. Unless the comment is totally off the wall criticisms can contain helpful ideas. It's wonderful to receive compliments so long as they are sincere and true. However, sometimes our critics have good insights for us. If we are sincere and ethical we will want to receive gentle words of correction. The sincere nonprofit operator sincerely wants to improve the organization they represent. One year I sent out 1,000 e-mails asking people to take time to provide feedback. One hundred people responded to the survey. Except for a few people that had worthless things to say I responded to each person. I found helpful tidbits of information and applied them to the Christian radio network, that I was operating. I thanked each person and regarded each comment as a helpful insight for improving operations. Almost a year to the day later I sent out a survey again to approximately 1000 people. I had acted on most of the suggestions throughout the previous year. This time, however most of the surveys came back with commendations. There were very few things practically speaking to correct. I share this information with modesty, saying that the listeners had valuable suggestions the previous year and listening to them was well worth the effort.

Gimmicks and ploys eventually will fall through. We need to be very careful that we are above reproach always. For example, when a nonprofit organization, is featuring a book and the contributor is asked to give a certain amount to receive said book the actual value of the book needs to be deducted from the donation. In other words, if the charity advertises that those who donate $30 and above will receive a hardcover book, and typically the hardcover book is worth $12 the charitable receipt is to indicate a donation of $18. The government is very leery about art donations. Someone may paint a picture and donate it to an organization and think that they have given a million-dollar masterpiece.

For example, let's say a painting of sunflowers in a field to some people looks like the work of grade four students. However, art critics who confer with one another and confirm that the value of said painting is worth hundreds of thousands of dollars can authenticate the amount. A charitable receipt is issued only when objective opinions confer what is the value of the artwork. If that painting is donated to a nonprofit organization and the charity auctions it the painter may be receipted for the agreed-upon value that has been confirmed by two or three noted art critics in that genre of painting. Similarly, some organizations receipt people who donate old cars. This is a worthwhile fundraising event. Not unless, however there is an agreed upon method of determining what the value of the old car is. There needs to be two or three people in the field of car sales to help ensure that the practices of the nonprofit organization are above reproach.

In the book, *Fundraising Principles and Practice* by Adrian Sargent and Jen Shang we begin to realize the importance of studying donor behavior. On page 164 they talk about psychographics. They cite Strategic Business Insights. See www.strategicbusinessinsights.com/vals Just as in for-profit companies where understanding customers is critical to marketing, so too is understanding donors critical to fundraising.

VALS stands for values, attitudes and lifestyles. It was developed in 1978 by a social scientist and consumer futurist named Arnold Mitchell. He used a combination of sociology and psychology to arrive at his conclusions. Mitchell used statistics to categorize American consumers. There are eight or nine primary groups, depending on how you look at it. Some of the population are referred to as survivors. Others are sustainers, and another group is labelled as "belonging". Some are called emulators, and others are achievers. The groups with the most resources are innovators, thinkers, believers, achievers, and strivers. These consumers are on the leading edge of change and have the highest incomes. They generally have high esteem and abundant resources. They can indulge in self orientations. Image is important to them because they like to express their independence. Their consumer choices are directed toward the" finer things in life." Fund raising efforts are best directed to self motivated, entrepreneurial type people because they generally have the most disposable income. Followers, are often working for someone else and don't have as much money to give to an organization comparatively speaking.

The category referred to as thinkers are consumers with plenty of resources. This group is motivated by ideals. They are mature, responsible, well-educated professionals. Their leisure activity centers on their phones. They are well informed about what goes on in the world and are open to new ideas and social change. They have high incomes but are practical consumers and rational decision-makers.

Next, we have believers. These consumers are the low resource group. They are conservative and predictable consumers who favor local products and established brands. Their lives are centered on family, community and the nation. They have modest incomes. While a charitable organization should not overlook these people, reasonable resources and a significant amount of time is justifiably spent on attracting business owners, and self-employed people. The purpose is self-evident. Generally, people who have their own companies are more likely to be able to give substantial gifts to charitable organization. The nonprofit can do much more with a few sizable well-planned gifts instead of expending hordes of time and attention on tiny gifts that may not add up in the end.

Let's look at the group referred to as the achievers. These consumers are the high resource people and are motivated by achievement. They are successful work oriented people who get their satisfaction from their jobs and families. They are politically conservative and respect authority and the status quo. They favor established products and services that show off their success to their peers. Next are strivers. These consumers are the low resource group. They have values like achievers but have fewer economic, social and psychological resources. Style is extremely important to them as they strive to emulate people they admire.

Mailing lists can be purchased so that a targeted group of people can be reached with appeals. For example, an organization that seeks to save wildlife can pick up on those who identify themselves as being animal lovers. Facebook allows people to post their likes and dislikes. Their profiles identify them per their hobbies, interests, etc. paid Facebook posts by a charitable organization can be targeted to a certain demographic in an area. The same can be done with Google ad words so that when people do a search on a topic, a charitable organization can be brought to the forefront. Print media has suffered serious setbacks because of the measurable results from advertising utilizing social media and search engines. Wise nonprofit managers will do well to utilize such methods to attract new donors.

Is it ethical for a nonprofit organization to utilize the science of psychology to identify the most likely donors? Is it ethical to target certain groups of people with specific marketing campaigns to elicit donor response? What do you think of holding a golf tournament for example and asking well-known people to invite people who would want to be associated with them? For example, a company owner who donates $10,000 to a charitable cause challenges other associates in that field to match his gift.

What do you think about buying mailing lists that have identified certain categories of people who may be particularly interested in your nonprofit organization? Does this create an unfair advantage or is it smart fundraising? What do you think about positioning a nonprofit?

It is important that every director of development write a case statement for appealing to potential donors. The legendary fundraiser Maurice Gurin (1985) recalls in his autobiography the case statement he wrote in 1958 for Princeton University's $53 million campaign. The statement, which was drafted at the height of the Cold War with the Soviet Union is titled, *Not for Princeton Alone*, and begins with, "It is now conceivable, technologically, to annihilate a continent or to rid mankind of disease. How we respond to this challenge (and to others of equal urgency) will determine how we live or whether we die" (Gurin, 1985, p. 109).

This was certainly appealing to people's sense of unrest during the Cold War. It addressed an underlying concern in society that American not be taken over by the Communists. Was this manipulation or meeting a need? People need to feel something when an appeal is made. If there is nothing felt, they most likely will not give. You need to present the need and show how their gift will solve a problem you have presented. Education through

Princeton was perceived as helping to defend America from Soviet invasion and better the world. Whether this was accurate was debateable. What is not up for debate was that it resulted in huge sums of money being donated to Princeton.

In Gurin's case statement for Princeton was America presented as a good nation and the USSR as evil? Not necessarily. This is not outside the scope of our discussion. Do you consider this ethical fundraising or perhaps have we taken the quote out of context? Was Gurin trying to paint the Russians as evil and the Americans as righteous or was he simply trying to inspire greatness? The threat of nuclear annihilation was real. Bear in mind it had only been a little over a decade since the US helped rid Europe of the crazed egotist Hitler. This was still prominent in people's thinking. WW II has resulted in disease and mass destruction. Had the same energy of the Nazi war machine been put into saving lives instead of destroying them the world would have been a much better place. This was the backdrop for his appeal. The question begs asking; was it ethical to phrase it as he did or would you consider it emotional manipulation? When Greenpeace shows pictures of destitute animals is it playing on people's heart strings or is it a factual presentation?

It is paramount that we have nonprofit organizations. The reason is because there are many social needs. The for-profit sector is focused on making money. the government cannot meet all the needs of society. We need to have the nonprofit sector otherwise many people would be in dire situations or situations worse than what they are facing. Nonprofits are often looked down upon because they ask for money. This is unfair. By the fact, they are meeting societal needs indicates they need special funding.

Not all activities are going to yield profit. Helping a senior citizen receive their daily insulin is not going to yield a profit. Conducting a breakfast program at school may not turn a profit either. However, the sad reality is that many children come from poor families who cannot provide proper nutrition. When children arrive at school with empty stomachs they cannot concentrate on their schoolwork. This sort of program requires private donations.

Nonprofit Issues and Management

The operators of nonprofit organization should not be ashamed to make appeals for funding. They need to stay focused on the good they are doing and how society would be deprived if they had to cease their operations.

Donor acquisition or development can be very costly. Direct mail, advertising, etc. can require substantial amounts of money. Potentially a significant percentage of the contributions can be used for these types of costs rather than directly going to fulfill the charitable objectives of the nonprofit organization. The cost to acquire a donor can be quite high relatively speaking. However, are there donors who otherwise would not be reached and hence the overall good far outweighs the costs to acquire new donors?

Routinely, a nonprofit need to examine the amount of money it is using to acquire donations. For example, is it costing $30 per donor to acquire new contributors who on average throughout the year give $300 each? A 10% donor acquisition cost may be deemed by some as too high. This is a subjective opinion. Each Board of Directors for individual charities must determine what for that organization is an ethical percentage of the contributions that can be utilized for administrative costs.

A downtown inner city mission does well to point out what it costs to provide a meal for a homeless person and a nice shelter. For example, the cost may be $2.49. People can identify with this and feel good about helping someone. The charity may then go on to multiply that by 30 days and asked the daughter to be a monthly contributor to help people.

There are good feelings associated with donating. A charity does well to identify these feelings and present the sense of satisfaction that people have by giving to charity. Direct mail is one of the most effective ways of raising money. Quite often, social media simply helps to heighten people's awareness. However, in terms of actual dollars that come from Facebook campaigns, e-mail campaigns, etc. is quite minimal in comparison to letters sent to potential donor's homes. It's important for people to receive correspondence from the charitable organization eleven months out of the year. This keeps the charity current in people's thinking so when they are prepared to donate. they readily think of the charity that has been most prominent month by month. Direct marketing is very effective because it reaches people in their homes. It's important for a nonprofit to measure response, and the cost per response.

It is important to present a case. There needs to be a one-page fundraising letter. Electronic fundraising is of value today. It is important to keep the appeal short and simple. Make it compelling. E-mail fundraising is of moderate benefit. It needs to be consistent and relevant. The nonprofit organization needs to be sure that the potential donor can opt out of receiving future e-mails. Telephone solicitation often irritates the homeowner.

It is important to thank the donors to show accountability and transparency. People give to charities for assorted reasons and mainly because they want to meet critical needs. They believe the nonprofit is providing an important service that government fails to do. Other reasons include identifying with the cause, religious convictions, etc. Some people will not give when they feel the charity has asked for money too often or the donor questions the integrity of the charitable organization.

It is paramount that the nonprofit build constituency. Relationships are essential to the longevity and success of any nonprofit. To do this there must be effective communication. The nonprofit must clearly present its vision. A clear, concise mission statement is an absolute necessity. A relationship of trust is built with the donor.

If nonprofits ceased to exist society would be greatly inhibited. Collectively, America's charitable organizations are referred to as the third largest sector after business and government. Charities principally receive money from the following sources: individuals, bequests, foundations and corporations. Nonprofits generally fall into the following categories: religion, education, health/hospitals, and human services.

There are several methods and techniques of fundraising: annual giving, major giving, estate or planned gifts. Major gifts generally come from endowments, corporations and foundations. Annual giving can result from special benefits and events, membership, direct mail. The professional fundraiser is ethical and virtuous; wholehearted, persistent and impartial. The purpose of fundraising is more than marketing, or the promotion of values.

The purpose of a strategy for raising money is precisely to enable the nonprofit institution to carry out its mission. Many nonprofit people have now changed the term they use from fundraising to fund development. Fundraising is asking for money because the need is so great. Fund development is creating a constituency which develops the organization because it deserves it. It means developing a membership that participates through giving." Friendships and relationships are essential. It is important that the donors have confidence in the organization. The organization must have a good public image. The organization must be fiscally sound and well managed, too.

Philanthropy is misunderstood. People give for various reasons. We should never try to motivate people to get out of guilt. People give because they identify with a cause and the charitable objectives. They see a human need and want to help to meet that need. It gives them a sense of meaning and purpose in life. People may give because they are spiritually or religiously motivated. Recognize donors have a sense of satisfaction when they give. To raise money, you need to inform and educate people. Is very effective to tell stories and repeat them often. Give real-life examples of lives who are being changed by the charitable organization. It is essential that you have earned the confidence and trust of the potential donor.

Huntsinger, provides several important components necessary for an effective fundraising letter. They are as follows:

number one - make everything easy to read, use short paragraphs and indent the first line of every paragraph. Number two - use underlining to capture the eye. Number three - avoid. letters that are difficult to read and give the feeling that you are shopping. Number four - keep your lines short, and leave lots of white space. Wide margins increase readership. Number five - use dashes instead of commas-at times-to break up the routine. Number six - be sure to give an attention grabber on each page. Seven - use large typefaces. Only 1% of the population has perfect eyesight. Appeal letters will cultivate, educate and inspire friends and donors to continue their faithful support.

A nonprofit organization needs to have a well-defined purpose. It needs to be an efficient organization with a realistic timetable. The director of development needs to have a clear case statement. Tell stories of lives that are improved. People give to change lives. Not to pay for salaries or buy equipment.

In the book, entitled Achieving Excellence in Fundraising, Volume 26, authors Timothy Seiler, Eva Aldrich and Eugene Tempel provide helpful information for structuring fund raising. It is important to have an overview of the entire development plan. For example, a well-funded nonprofit will focus not only on individual modest sized gifts but specifically target large annual gifts from a foundation or endowment. It is important for a charitable organization to emphasize what distinguishes it from other charitable organizations. It also needs to demonstrate how the charity is accountable. A clear mission, goals and objectives need to be presented. The charity or nonprofit needs to show how it is relevant to society's needs. Colleges, universities, hospitals, operas, art museums, rehabilitation programs, are all examples of nonprofits. Successful campaigns need to focus on clearly stated goals, communicating effectively, and demonstrating accountability, and transparency to donors. There needs to be a bond with the donors.

If the nonprofit is to remain viable, or even to expand it will need to have people who include them in their wills, requests, annuities, charitable trusts, and pooled income funds. There can be planned gifts of life insurance, estates, and planned gifts. Not only is direct mail essential for funding nonprofits so too are major gifts necessary.

It is easy to submit the rationale that many gifts will be easier to secure than the two larger gifts. It will require that 250 $100 gifts substitute for a $25,000 gift. This means that 1,000 prospects must be solicited to secure 250 gifts. The top 10% of the gifts received during the annual fund have the potential to produce 60% of the money required to meet the goal. The next 20% of gifts will count for 15 to 25% of the money required. The remaining 70% of gifts will cover the remaining 15 to 25% of funds required.

A person can expend a lot of time focusing on small gifts. Small gifts are to be received with gratitude, particularly if a person in a lower income bracket is getting proportionately more than, one might realize. It may be very noble to focus on small gifts. However, a lot of energy and time can be spent acquiring small donations. Albeit large donations require a lot of work. However, in the long run it will help the nonprofit succeed when a few substantial donations are raised.

Scrutinized and analyze the gift potential in the donor base. The following questions should be asked: how many donors give annually? What is the frequency of the gift? Once a year, twice a year or more often? How many donors give monthly? What is the level of giving? Do they give $10,000 or more a year, $1,000 $5000, $5,000-$1,000? $1,000-$500 or less than $500? Is there a pattern of the gift being repeated, but not upgraded over the years? Is a regular request made that the gift will be upgraded? Do the records identify donors who give regularly to the annual fund, as well as make special-purpose, capital or endowment gifts? Is there a specific person identified as the solicitor of the gift? What is the pattern of giving by staff members, trustees and members of advisory councils or do they not give? This vital information is an essential part of the fundraisers knowledge. This information will enable the person planning the fundraising program to identify the potential gifts required by the gift range chart.

Face-to-face visits with potential donors can seem very intimidating. However, when one concentrates on the tremendous benefit the nonprofit is providing to society one need not feel embarrassed. Phone calls are not very effective because it is easy for people to say no over the telephone. One needs look over the donor support list and analyze asking this question, "Who of these people are potential donors in the annual campaign and who may possibly increase their donation over the previous year? It's very important to bond with constituents. Be certain that donors have access to information about the operations of programs. Be accountable and transparent.

Major gifts are also known as gifts of significance. Securities, valuable art, tangible property, multiyear pledges, charitable trusts, annuities, etc. all need to be considered. Henry Rosso said, "Fundraising is the gentle art of teaching people the joy of giving." It is important for the fundraiser to recognize what motivates potential major benefactors. One must know the passion of the potential benefactor and what motivates them to give. "Fundraising professionals are not selling products; rather, they are promoting visions and possibilities for the betterment of humankind." The fundraiser can ask the major donor, what they value? A wise development officer will take close notes. It is important to establish trust and assure the philanthropist their information will remain confidential. The development officer may ask, what were the major influences in his or her life? Who particularly inspired you and what kind of legacy would you like to leave after you depart from this life? What is the most satisfying gifted you have made and why? Which of the nonprofits you support does the best job of keeping you involved and aware of what is happening? What kind of reports do you want as a donor? How do you prefer to be informed about the opportunity to give to a charity; by e-mail, by phone call or by letter?

It is important to cultivate a relationship of trust with the donor and to help them see that they are making an investment in lives. Tell stories which are like windows to show what's happening. The donor must catch the vision of what the charitable organization is seeking to accomplish.

Nonprofit Issues and Management

Help people see how the nonprofit that they are giving to is changing the world around them. More and more philanthropists are wanting to be sure that their money is being put to good use. There are different kinds of philanthropists the same as there are different kinds of investors. Angel investors are not involved in the day-to-day operations of the Startup company. However, some investors want not only a percentage of the shares but a say in how things are covered. Some donors may have few expectations and others may want to sit as members of the Board of Directors. They want to be sure that their money is being used properly.

There are venture capitalists who are willing to take risks. The way to appeal to some donors is on this basis; that charity is on the cutting edge of society pioneering new methods of eliciting change. This may appeal to the entrepreneurial type. If one is expecting a lawyer to give then present a well reasoned case. If one is expecting an accountant to give them one needs to provide financial spreadsheets and a demonstration of accountability. However, the best use of time for the fundraiser maybe to present his case to entrepreneurs, investors, and self-employed people.

Those who invest in the stock market may see a charitable organization the same as when they get their stock portfolio. They were willing to take some risks and if they see that charity is growing and developing they may want to get behind the initiative. The development officer must have a creative mind. He needs to present the one year, three year and even five year goals of the charitable organization. This will attract a certain type of donor. While we appeal to the logical side of people we also need to appeal to their emotions.

We need to help people have a good feeling about the benefit of the gift. If it touches their heartstrings it will lead to their purse strings. Some self-made people may see themselves as having brought themselves up by their own bootstraps. They feel that nobody really gave them a break in life so why should they help others. Don't waste too much time on these kinds of people. Look for generous, sensitive, hearted people who want to make a difference in the world around them. Be certain to study how their business succeeded and find out why they became a success. Appeal to them on that basis. Show them that the charity seeks to model and emulate similar qualities, i.e. arduous work, creativity, thinking outside the box, ingenuity.

A capital campaign is an intensive fundraising effort designed to raise a specified sum of money within a defined period to meet the varied asset building needs of an organization. This may mean the construction of a new building, renovation or enlargement of existing buildings, purchase of land, acquisition of equipment, etc. A table of gifts is needed for various levels of giving.

Nonprofits are necessary for strengthening society. They provide a service. In so doing, the government allows for special tax privileges. To carry out their functions they need to solicit funding. This requires transparency. There is a document known as the donor Bill of Rights and code of ethics. In Canada, we have what is referred to as the Canadian Association of gift planners. The public often puts officers, directors, and fundraisers under a microscope. It is very important that the charity and employees protect their reputation. There must be no impropriety.

In her book, Ethical Decision Making and Fundraising. Marilyn Fisher discusses what is required to act with integrity. One needs independent judgment, responsibility and moral courage. A good reputation is often linked with integrity. The reputation of a nonprofit organization is to be guarded always because it is one of his most important assets, if not its most important asset. If there are any conflicts of interests they must be avoided at all costs. People should be appointed to the board based on their character, and sincerity.

James Greenfield wrote about the rights of donors. Professional fundraising practitioners began to build a set of principles known today as the donor Bill of Rights. Their goals included to assist donors in making decisions about charities, believing, informed decision-making would assist donors and charities in forging stronger, more productive relationships that would ultimately benefit the recipients of charitable support. Donors should expect to be informed of the organizations mission, of the way the organization intends to use the donated resources and of its capacity to use the donations effectively for their intended purposes.

It's very important for a charitable organization to have a clear mission statement to guide it so that donors know specifically how their money is being used. If the donor gives a certain amount of money thinking it will be used for a certain cause and it turns out that the donation is being used for something altogether different than this creates an issue of mistrust. It is very important that the charitable organization use the money specifically for what is its intended purpose. The public is trusting that the charitable organization is using the money for its intended purposes and not for the benefit of the directors or employees. The donor also has a right to expect that their information will be kept confidential. The donor has the right to expect to know who is sitting on the Board of Directors. The donor has a right to know whether the people carrying out the purposes of the charity are volunteers or employees. They also have the right to know what the financial statements are. They need to be sure that their gifts are being used for the purposes for which they were given. They also have the right to have their names deleted from mailing lists whenever they decide. The charitable organization should allow for regular feedback to find out how people perceive the nonprofit organization is doing. They need to find out whether people are satisfied and allow for questions. There must be a bond of trust between the donors and the charity.

Greenfield, James M. *Fundraising fundamentals: A guide to annual giving for professionals and volunteers*. Vol. 210. John Wiley & Sons, 2004.

Seiler, Timothy L., Eva E. Aldrich, and Eugene R. Tempel. *Achieving excellence in fundraising*. Vol. 26. John Wiley & Sons,

Jeff Lutes

2010.

Chapter 3. Comparing Nonprofit and For-profits

Companies that are set up with shareholders and pay dividends pay corporate tax. Nonprofit companies do not pay tax, other than salary deductions for employees. When establishing a company one should not look at nonprofit status simply as a tax shelter. Nonprofit and for-profit companies have very different purposes. A for-profit company, as its name suggests, is for benefiting its owners and shareholders. A nonprofit company, such as a hospital or university may have an overarching purpose of benefiting society and helping people.

People who own shares or stock in a company have a say in how it is operated. This is in direct relation to the amount of money they have invested. It is reasonable to say that people who receive a service from a nonprofit organization or donate to said organization are the shareholders. The managers, vice presidents, presidents, etc. of a for-profit company are answerable to the investors. Similarly, the executive and supervisors of a nonprofit organization are answerable to the donors or quite possibly to the people who receive the service. The people who have purchased stock in a for-profit company expect a return on their investment. The people who make donations or receive a service from a nonprofit expect the objectives and mission will be fulfilled. When nonprofit organizations see themselves in this light they are likely to be more effective.

Investors are Shareholders in a For-profit Company	Donors should be regarded as important to a Nonprofit as a Investors are to a For-profit

Jeff Lutes

A company generally has a president, vice president and other executives who answer to the shareholders. Specifically, the chairman of the board represents the shareholders and major investors. The board hold the executive responsible who in turn supervise the staff. The president of a company must answer to the chairman of the board and provide reports. Similarly, in a nonprofit there should be a chairman of the board and other board members who hold a manager or president accountable. The employees answer to the president and should never go over this person's head to speak directly to the chairman of the board. They should work matters out with their supervisor. Nonprofit organizations cannot be haphazard in their operations and answer to no one. A nonprofit organization must have structure and accountability in order for it to be effective.

Chairperson   President   Employees

One of the main points that I want to establish is that it is not only for-profit companies that must exercise sound fiscal decisions, so too must nonprofits. Nonprofit companies, for all intents and purposes need to be operated similarly. Meaning, they need to exercise wise fiscal decisions. Many nonprofit organizations encounter grave difficulties because they take too much for granted. Just because they do not have shareholders, hungry for profit does not mean they should disregarded the importance of sound decisions. Regardless of whether the objective is to make a profit, both need to be operated with sound business principles.

By times those associated with the nonprofit organization can be quite idealistic and not fiscally grounded. The same as in a for-profit corporation monthly or quarterly cash flow statements need to be produced by the finance department along with an operating budget and other reports that help the nonprofit remain fiscally sound. The nonprofit must have a sound fiscal policy to govern how it spends money. Often there are difficult financial decisions that need to be made to keep the nonprofit on track. If the nonprofit is for example, a humanitarian organization it may be especially difficult to stay on target financially. Human need must not always be allowed to govern the decisions that are made. If the organization collapses financially then it will not be able to go on to help others in the future. Idealism is good so long as those in charge of a nonprofit do not lose touch with reality.

The role of nonprofits in society is a very important one. For example, hospitals are crucial for people's health. If they are not managed properly the level of healthcare can deteriorate causing serious ramifications. Particularly with government-funded or subsidized organizations, there is the possibility that if money is made available to meet the budget they can drift along. Often, people in government positions can be out of touch with the real world because they do not face the same constraints as their counterparts in the corporate world. If, for example, a for-profit company is not attracting new clientele and making sales it quickly goes out of business. This is not so for a hospital to continue because there will always be sick people in need of a medical treatment. Other checks and balances need to be in place when there is no sales quota, so to speak to meet.

Government funding is fine so long as the political party issuing the money stays in power. The next government may not hold the to the same sympathies or values. Therefore, it is often difficult for a nonprofit organization to receive bank financing. When the grant is up an organization that has become dependent on the source of money often collapses. It is important for a nonprofit to have a diverse portfolio of income sources. Nonprofit organizations need to be careful they do not allow themselves to fall into such a vulnerable place. Patrons, sponsors, etc. will help to diversify the support base so that if government funding is removed the organization does not cease to exist.

It is important to conduct surveys to allow people to express how they really feel about the nonprofit. Generally, there is always something to learn from negative criticism. Sometimes the feedback will be extreme and unreasonable. If a nonprofit is not selling anything, it needs a different way to measure effectiveness than for-profit companies. I have found e-mail surveys to be an efficient, convenient way for people to provide valuable insights on how to improve service. It is important to ask the right questions in the survey. Ask people about a new service that is being offered and whether they find it helpful, needs improvement or if they are indifferent.

A good survey is one that will tell us things we were not aware of; perhaps reveal things we don't want to hear and confirm the areas where we are doing well. Surveys build good relationships with donors and recipients of the service. It helps them to feel they are valued and appreciated. You can begin to recognize general trends and the overall needs of people by surveys. Feedback is valuable to be certain that a nonprofit is operating effectively. Surveys should be conducted at least annually to gain a sense as to whether the nonprofit is achieving its objectives.

One of the benefits of operating a nonprofit organization is that the focus can be on providing quality of service and not just turning a profit. With for-profit companies, sometimes the quality of workmanship deteriorates because of unrealistic sales quotas. A nonprofit organization may be less tempted to cut corners than a for-profit company. Working for a nonprofit can be very fulfilling because the focus can remain on caring for people and providing quality service. Those working in a for-profit company can become very frustrated and feel they are being used.

The biggest difference between nonprofit and for-profit is the reason why they exist. An example of a nonprofit organization is the World Wildlife Federation. If it were not for them some species would cease to exist. Inversely for-profit corporations have been accused by many as having a disregard for the environment because money is the key focus. This is not to say that for-profit corporations do not have a social conscience, as well. A nonprofit is not money driven. While money is needed, it is not part of the overall objective. Reasonable salaries, moderate expenses, etc. all go into the operation of the nonprofit. Nonprofit organizations do not exist to make money or reward shareholders. Rather the purpose of the nonprofit is to fulfill an objective or ideal.

Working for a nonprofit can be very rewarding. Generally, a nonprofit has high ideals and an employee can feel they are making a difference in the world. The person working at a nonprofit doesn't fall into the trap of thinking they are just working to line someone's pockets. It could be a sports association, a religious organization or a humanitarian effort; these are very noble purposes. This does not guarantee a higher level of job satisfaction on the part of employees but it can make a difference. Money is a motivator but it is not the best motivator. Knowing that you are helping people achieve ideals has greater fulfillment in the long run. This is not to say that nonprofits should take this for granted. Rather it is to say that nonprofits have an advantage in this area.

Nonprofits need to be careful they don't fall into the trap of ignoring the bottom fiscal line. They may think because they are not money motivated they do not need to adhere to sound financial policies. Similar business principles need to be enforced for nonprofits as for-profit corporations. If overspending occurs the nonprofit ceases to exist. Nonprofits similarly need to look at overhead, expenses and salaries, etc. because if the amount they are spending to carry out their objectives is more than what the organization can sustain it will grind to a halt. While a nonprofit does not report to shareholders with quarterly statements showing dividends it still needs to report to the Board of Directors to show how money is being used to achieve the objectives.

Nonprofits need to be entrepreneurial in terms of being open to new ways of doing things. They need to be innovative and cutting-edge. I recommend the book entitled *Enterprising Nonprofits: A Toolkit for Social Entrepreneurs by* J. Gregory Dees, Jed Emerson, and Peter Economy because it motivates and gives a sense of purpose for nonprofit organizations and their leaders. More than ever nonprofit leaders need to be entrepreneurs. Operating nonprofits has become increasingly complicated. Fiscal restraint means nonprofit organizations need to become increasingly enterprising. A solid case needs to be built why the nonprofit is worthy of donations and funding. People will give if there is a sense of personal fulfillment and satisfaction in donating to the organization. Nonprofits need to be results driven to maintain funding.

Entrepreneur is a French word meaning someone who undertakes. An entrepreneur is someone who finds better ways of doing things. Peter Drucker said the entrepreneur looks for change, responds to it and exploits it as an opportunity. Nonprofits need to be increasingly innovative in their ideas and approaches to carrying out their mandate. They need to be bold and carry out calculated risks to expand otherwise they risk ceasing to exist as an organization. Nonprofit organizations are not second rate places where people who cannot succeed in the business realm go for employment. If anything, the managers and employees of nonprofit organizations need to be wiser, and more resourceful than people in for-profit organizations to stay in operation.

Nonprofit organizations need to have people of action who are willing to try innovative ideas. They need to be able to act decisively and quickly as the need arises. People who work for a nonprofit organization need to be devoted and passionate about what they do because the obstacles facing them are greater than for-profit corporations. Without this commitment, the organization most likely will flounder and fallback. There needs to be a keen sense of mission and purpose to motivate the employees and workers of the nonprofit. Having a sense of purpose and goodwill will motivate employees to go further than employees in a for profit business.

Peter Drucker wrote an article entitled, *"What Businesses Can Learn from Nonprofits."* He begins by saying,

> The Girl Scouts, the Red Cross and pastoral charges are becoming America's management leaders. In two areas, strategy and the effectiveness of the board, they are practicing what most American businesses only preach. And in the most crucial area-the motivation and productivity of knowledge workers-they are truly pioneers, working out the policies and practices that business must learn tomorrow. Few people are aware that the nonprofit sector is by far America's largest employer.

He goes on to point out that as a rule nonprofits are more careful in the way they handle money than for-profit corporations. He speaks of the success of the Salvation Army in Florida helping to rehabilitate convicts when they come out of prison. The Girl Scouts help young ladies become confident, capable and people who not only respect themselves but others.

About Willow Creek, Drucker said,

> Bill Hybels, in his early twenties when he founded the church, chose the community because it had relatively few churchgoers, though the population was growing fast and churches were plentiful. He went from door to door asking, "Why don't you go to church?" Then he designed a church to answer the potential customers' needs: for instance, it offers full services on Wednesday evenings because many working parents need Sunday to spend with their children.

J. Gregory Dees was an adjunct professor of social entrepreneurship and nonprofit management at Duke University's Fuqua School of Business. He was the head of the Center for Advancement of Social Entrepreneurship (CASE) at Duke. He died at the age of 63 and during his lifetime he helped show how the theory and practice of entrepreneurship could be blended with social missions to tackle poverty, pollution and other global challenges in new, high-impact ways. *"Greg Dees was the pioneer in building social entrepreneurship as an academic field of study,"* said Maya Ajmera, a Duke alumna and founder of the Global Fund for Children. Sally Osberg, president and CEO of the Skoll Foundation, called Dees *"the rarest of academics. For two decades, his scholarship and teaching have been seminal to the field of social entrepreneurship; no one has been more influential, and no one more inspiring."*

Dees wrote in 2001,

> The idea of "social entrepreneurship" has struck a responsive chord. It is a phrase well suited to our times. It combines the passion of a social mission with an image of business-like discipline, innovation, and determination commonly associated with, for instance, the high-tech pioneers of Silicon Valley. The time is certainly ripe for entrepreneurial approaches to social problems. Many governmental and philanthropic efforts have fallen far short of our expectations. Major social sector institutions are often viewed as inefficient, ineffective, and unresponsive. Social entrepreneurs are needed to develop new models for a new century.

Challenging economic times require that nonprofits be managed by people willing to expand their horizons because funding can be scarce. Managing a nonprofit requires innovation, calculated risk taking and mental agility to circumvent the barrage of obstacles that stand in the way of being successful. Without this insightful leadership nonprofits are prone to stagnate and eventually dissolve. To succeed in the highly competitive age of globalization a nonprofit needs decisive leadership. This is generally associated with the for-profit sector however these qualities need to be carried over into the nonprofit sector. Dees wanted us to see that poverty, starvation, the spread of disease, etc. require decisive, intelligent, entrepreneurial type leaders in the nonprofit sector to overcome these huge social problems.

Nonprofit organizations need to be highly adaptive to the circumstances and economic climate surrounding them. They need to be industrious and innovative to stay afloat financially. Far from being second rate nonprofits that succeed do so because of exceptional managers. Agility in decision making, the ability to ascertain a situation, etc. are necessary qualities managers of nonprofits need to hone. Often those who succeed in the nonprofit sector could do equally well in a for-profit corporation because they already have the skill set necessary.

In *the Nonprofit: For-Profit Thinking for Nonprofit Success*, Steve Rothschild lists seven principles to help Nonprofits succeed. They are:

1. Have a clear and appropriate purpose
2. Measure what counts
3. Be market-driven
4. Create mutual accountability
5. Support personal empowerment
6. Create economic value from social benefit
7. Be learning driven

Currently if nonprofits are to attract government money, donations from philanthropists or otherwise they will need to be entrepreneurial, wise and innovative.

In his book, *Managing the Nonprofit Organization: Principles and Practices,* Peter F. Drucker highlights the importance of nonprofits having a clear mission statement. Nonprofits exist to bring about change in individuals and society. If the nonprofit loses sight of its mission statement, then it becomes ineffective. It is not enough to simply have good intentions. A person may be very committed to the cause of the nonprofit, however that will only carry the nonprofit so far. Effective, decisive leadership is needed for nonprofit organizations to stay afloat. The same sound business principles and wisdom that apply to for-profit companies need to be used in nonprofit organizations.

I'm not trying to say is that it is always the case that a manager in the nonprofit sector can do equally well in the for-profit sector. Neither am I trying to say that a manager in the for-profit sector could be equally effective in the nonprofit sector. Most definitely there are different mindsets for each sector. The point I am trying to make is effective managerial strategies apply in both sectors. What makes this good sense in a for-profit corporation should carry over in the management of a nonprofit organization. By virtue of the fact that a nonprofit organization it is in operation to achieve certain ideals and objectives that are different from profit motivated company is proof enough that managers do not always easily transition from one sector to the other. If a for-profit company would not overspend its resources it needs to be equally true of a charitable organization.

Effective managerial strategies apply in both sectors.

For-profit corporations exist to make money while nonprofit organizations are instituted to benefit society. To fulfill their function, they require private contributions, government grants, money from foundations, corporate philanthropy and bequests. For-profit corporations rely on competitiveness in the market, superior quality of their product, etc. No one owns a nonprofit organization while a for-profit corporation is owned by the shareholders.

This is not to say that a nonprofit should be unconcerned with finances and profitability. Any profits need to be utilized within the year to help carry out the objectives of the organization. Special provisions are made to set aside some of the profits for larger projects in ensuing years. There are many similarities between nonprofits and for-profit corporations and basically it comes down to one difference; what is done with the profit at the end of the year? Is it given out as a dividend to stockholders or is it retained in the organization to carry out objectives as set out in the constituting documents?

We need to have nonprofit organizations because healthcare should be for example be available to all people. Saving wildlife may have little tangible benefit in the immediate however in the long run it is necessary for the survival of humans. If it is an organization like Boy Scouts, it's hard to put a tangible price tag on helping lives. We should not look at nonprofit organizations as having lesser importance because they are not in operation to show huge profits. The success of a nonprofit is often difficult to measure. It is measured in changed lives which is priceless.

There are those who work in the nonprofit sector who have a low opinion of themselves because they think their job is less viable than their counterparts in the for-profit sector. If anything, they should think of themselves in a better light because they are often working with limited resources. We gauge our success or failure too much by a financial spreadsheet. We think our value is measured by sales and huge profits. Employees in the nonprofit sector can hold their heads high knowing they are making a difference in people's lives.. They are often doing more with less and surviving in a very difficult economic environment. Our sense of purpose should not come from the size of our paycheck.

Universities, hospitals, organizations that rescue women and children, cancer research foundations, Doctors without Borders, The Rotary Club, The Sierra Club, Samaritan's Purse, The Red Cross, World Wildlife Fund, museums and the list goes on of nonprofit organizations that benefit humanity. It is a noble and high calling to work for a nonprofit organization. The important work they do requires highly skilled and intelligent employees. There is nothing second-rate about nonprofits when we compare them with for-profit corporations. The same fortitude, hard work, and commitment that goes into making a company profitable needs to be devoted to nonprofits to make them successful and effective.

Chapter 4. Long Term Viability for Nonprofits

It's one thing to start a nonprofit but it's another to maintain its viability over the long-term. Organizations must constantly be reinventing themselves and keeping up on the latest technology. Strategizing and coming up with new and more efficient methods of achieving its objectives are paramount for the survival of a nonprofit organization. In this chapter, we will learn methods for long term viability from strategic planning to visionary leadership. It will encompass subjects such as donor retention, feedback and staying true to the mission statement or purpose of the nonprofit. In short, any nonprofit can experience long term viability when it stays true to its founding principles, yet keeps up with the times and has a clear direction set by strategic planning.

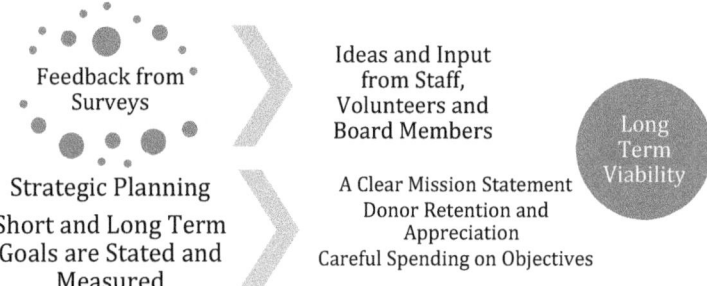

It is important for managers and boards of nonprofit organizations to help everyone understand what are the goals and objectives. It helps employees and volunteers stay focused when they know the clear purpose of the nonprofit organization. It is important to prioritize so that a nonprofit organization can focus its energies to succeed. Strategic goals help everyone in the organization to understand what their role and part is to help bring about success. Both short-term and long-term goals need to be set for the organization to move ahead. It is important to have a timetable as to when you expect these goals to be achieved, otherwise the organization may flounder.

In addition to setting goals, plans on how to implement them need to be established, as well. However, before setting goals a feasibility study needs to be conducted to be certain they are realistic and achievable. There must be ways to monitor the progress toward the achievement of these goals, too. Goals need to be attainable, specific and time sensitive. For example, a nonprofit may set a goal of attaining one hundred new donors in the coming year. It is not enough to simply set the goal, steps to achieve the goal need to be established. So, in the case of 100 new donors an organization may say they will mount a strategic advertising campaign, attend conferences and set up a booth, ask donors to give names of potential donors, etc. It would be helpful to break it down into quarters so that in the first quarter of the new year twenty-five new donors are acquired.

It stands to reason the people with the best ideas for improvement are those who are closest to the organization. Collectively their ideas can bring about tremendous change. Employees, donors and volunteers need to have a sense their voices are being heard and their ideas are integrated into the plan. This gives them a sense of ownership so they exhibit more dedication. Often, employees are intimidated about bringing their suggestions to their employer for fear of reprisal. If there is an open atmosphere that rewards creativity, volunteers and employees will have some of the best ideas for improvement. Polls and surveys can be conducted where people, if necessary can make anonymous comments. In some cases, it may be necessary to have a third person come in to ask for input so that the workers feel less intimidated. Never underestimate the intelligence of the people working with you.

It has been said advice is worth what you pay for it. Generally, people with decades of experience in the field are good resource people. It is wise to ask them for their input and they should be paid for their advice. Why make a mistake when you can avoid it in the first place because of counsel from people who have learned from the past? Research a topic, contact people with experience, conduct feasibility studies, etc. These helps to ensure the long-term viability of the nonprofit.

People must be free to make mistakes and allowed to experiment. If employees are so tightly regulated they are not able to expand in their field they will become interested. I advise having set tasks, but allowing a portion of the work day for creativity and an interchange of ideas. Not only does this keep minds fresh but it also gives a sense of empowerment to employees. If people feel respected and appreciated for their brilliance, not only do they help the organization improve, but they are more apt to work long-term. Employee turnover can cause tremendous setbacks for an organization.

Prevent secondary items from competing with primary ones. In other words, don't be so caught up in issues of lesser importance that the overall main objectives are neglected. Keep a task list and scrutinize what deserves your time. Time management courses are helpful because they increase productivity. Scheduling appointments instead of allowing for interruptions is an efficient use of time. Working in blocks of time and grouping tasks together increases efficiency instead of starting and stopping jobs.

Networking can be very helpful. Be certain that you are always obtaining new information in your field. Attend conferences and tradeshows to hear keynote speakers and visit the booths of distributors coming out with new products. Constantly exchange ideas with people in your field so you can be effective and relevant. Take every opportunity to learn and glean new ideas. This is a way to stay ahead of trends and remain viable. Stagnation and a refusal to grow will spell certain demise. Nonprofits need to be constantly evolving and reinventing themselves to keep up with changes in society.

It is important to be attending seminars, and other opportunities for learning. It's beneficial to learn from other people in the industry or feel that you represent. One of the sure strategies to ensure the long-term viability of a nonprofit is for the Board of Directors, managers, employees to read books in the field and constantly be acquiring new ideas. The famous seven last words of any organization are, "We never did it that way before." Trying innovative ideas, and learning from leaders in the field will help ensure long-term viability.

Technology is changing so quickly that if the company does not keep abreast of what is happening it may soon find itself replaced by others who can perform the same service cheaper and faster. It is keenly essential to have a superb website because it is the modern-day equivalent of a front window display and a bright sign for a store on the main street in the past. Social media is a great benefit, but it should not be overrated. While it helps to build brand recognition regular mail is still one of the most effective ways to stay in contact with constituents.

Donor acquisition is one of the most important aspects of operating a charity. Effective marketing can help attract new donors with pictures that grab the attention of prospects. The use of social media for advertising is helpful, as well. Ask people who are presently giving to suggest the names of people the nonprofit may approach to become a supporter. It is important to build brand recognition whenever possible. Clearly and concisely present your mission statement to potential donors. Communicate well how the donations are used effectively and give examples of the difference the gifts make. Use stories and examples of people whose lives have been changed by the nonprofit organization. This will appeal to the heart of potential donors and encourage them to get behind the organization.

Nonprofits need to work especially hard to build confidence and be trustworthy. This comes by showing accountability and responding to viable criticisms. A nonprofit organization needs to be continually showing that it is viable otherwise or it will go out of existence. It needs to show that it is dynamic and in touch with the needs of people. Donors can be fickle and if their questions are not answered they may quickly choose to give to another organization. There needs to be transparency in financial reporting and operations.

The vision and objectives of the nonprofit need to be clearly articulated to both employees and potential donors. It needs to be succinct and easily communicated. All decisions need to be run through the grid of this question; how is this helping us to fulfill our objectives and mandate? The organization needs to be streamlined so that it is efficient and this will help to ensure long-term viability. This is in keeping with brand recognition and keeping the name of the organization in front of potential donors continuously. The name of the organization needs to be synonymous with quality and excellence.

One of the most important ways to ensure the long-term viability of a nonprofit is to develop high donor retention rate. If appreciation is shown to donors, clear communication, transparency, and other important facts a donor may continue with an organization for many years. Building a relationship with donors is crucial so they feel connected to the organization. Generally, if people feel their donation is appreciated, that it is being used properly, and the organization is achieving results people will continue to give. If there is a disconnect with donors the dollars will soon drop off.

If a nonprofit organization gains 100 new donors in a year and in year two, only fifty of them give a second time the donor retention rate is 50%. If there is a low donor retention rate, then immediate steps need to be taken. It's important to know why a person started giving in the first place and continue to do what attracted the person. It's extremely important to build a relationship with donors to make them feel valued and respected. Personal "thank you" letters, remembering someone on their birthday, etc. are effective ways to promote donor retention. It is very important that the charity communicate well with the supporters by regular newsletters, banquets, etc. Calling on donors, remembering specifics about them, such as their children, being there help the supporter to feel they are integral part of the organization. If they are in the hospital visit them, and other such acts of kindness will help donors stay with a ministry or organization for a long time.

Donor fatigue can be a very serious matter when people have been tapped too many times for too much money. They need to be assured their funds are being used responsibly and have measurable results. If people begin to lose interest donations will drop off. Contact with donors needs to be continually so they do not lose interest. If too much is asked of donors, they may become discouraged and walk away. It is crucial that an atmosphere of appreciation is always exhibited. Gifts are very helpful in maintaining trust between the giver and the organization. These can be in the form of fruit baskets, books, cards, etc.

Donor fatigue is a very serious matter for a nonprofit organization. When people no longer donate to charities who once were committed supporters it is indicative of underlying problems. The directors and managers of a nonprofit organization need to fight against apathy and indifference. This can happen when the same message is given over and over to supporters. Eventually, they feel no real sense of urgency to give. If a nonprofit venture into areas that donors are not interested in there will be a drop in donations. If too much pressure is put on the donor for monthly pledges or the amounts are too large they will vote by not giving.

The way to fight donor fatigue is by showing the urgency of giving. Building a strong relationship with donors is very important and receiving feedback from them. Those who operate a nonprofit need to constantly be looking at how they are communicating with supporters. If the donors are passionate about the charity they will never become tired of giving to it. This kind of passion needs to be fostered always. Ask the individuals how they want the charity to communicate with them? Some do not want to receive letters and assure you they will support the nonprofit organization regardless. They will give you if they are interested. Some prefer e-mail or a phone call to stay in touch with the charity of their choice. It is always important to let supporters know how their money has been used and the results.

Bradie Sheehan in a 2011 Honors project for Grand Valley State University entitled, "*Helping Your Nonprofit Organization Stay Viable During Tough Economic Times*" had this to say regarding long term viability,

> Cultivating relationships with long term donors can help ensure their continued support helping an organization maintain stable funding. It also opens the door for conversations about planned giving.... Nonprofits can approach donors with which they have relationships and

talk about the possibility of posthumous giving. If the donor has been a longtime giver they may be very open to the idea of including the organization in their will. Since seventy percent of people do not have wills this is another large opportunity for nonprofits. Many people may be willing to leave part of their estate to charity but they just have not thought about it. Nonprofits can take advantage of this fact with long-time donors.

It is crucial that a charitable organization have a tremendous website that makes it very easy for people to give online. Giving online is very important and a website must be viewed easily on a cell phone because many people will give directly using their mobile device. The text and pictures need to be seen clearly on a cell phone before people will utilize the donate button. It is also important that a nonprofit have a strong Facebook presence and even utilize it as a method of advertising to attract donors and supporters.

Endowments are set up for the long-term sustainability of a nonprofit. An endowment is a financial asset, in the form of a donation made to a nonprofit group consisting of investment funds or other property. Investments can be made on behalf of the charitable organizations so it receives the benefit of the residual income. It can be in the form of a Guaranteed Investment Certificate, Mutual Funds, Stock in a company, etc. Roman Emperor and Stoic philosopher Marcus Aurelius in A.D. 176 endowed chairs for each of the major schools of philosophy: Platonism, Aristotelianism, Stoicism and Epicureanism. A University needs endowments to be certain it is not reliant on tuition from students. When the student is treated like a customer the standards of education begin to fall. A professor needs to be free to research and teach without trying to appease anyone. The Chair they fill needs to be fully funded and to do this there must be endowments.

A charitable organization can encourage regular donors to consider a life insurance policy that would be paid out to the charity. If new donors are not coming along as quickly as old donors are passing away the charity will fade into oblivion. It can continue to fulfill its objectives if donors are making payments on policies and being receipted for a portion of the premiums. The charity owns the policy and the donor makes the payments so that upon death, the organization receives the payout.

Matching support from a philanthropist is a way to ensure the long-term viability of a nonprofit organization. People with smaller gifts are enthused to know that the power of their gift is doubled because of the philanthropist. This helps the rich benefactor realize they are not the only one who is making a commitment. This also keeps the nonprofit organization from becoming too dependent upon rich individuals who make large donations. It ensures the responsibilities spread relative to people's income.

Some corporations are learning it is good for business to support nonprofits. Clients and customers like to know that a corporation is giving back to the community. Companies that have a social conscience are often patronized by the public. Wise heads of nonprofits can avail themselves of this opportunity to partner with for-profit corporations. The advertising can work both ways;

the nonprofit uses its network to publicize the names of corporations that are helping it and corporations publicize that a portion of their customers' sales go to help the nonprofit organization achieve its objectives. This is a win-win situation and most importantly a winning situation for the people who benefit from the services of the nonprofit organization.

A nonprofit organization needs to be sure that it has applied a financial margin for error and that projects are not costing more than first anticipated. Basically, more needs to be coming in than going out for the initiatives of the organization. There needs to be an assessment tool to ascertain if the project is viable and should be undertaken at that time. If the organization is overextended and underfunded it will cease to exist. A nonprofit organization needs to have clearly defined boundaries so it does not become defunct. Scrutiny of projects, ensuring the necessary level of funding is in place and other checks and balances will help ensure the organization continues for many years to come.

It is crucial that a nonprofit organization has a very specific operating budget and works strictly within the confines of this valuable tool. Financial projections need to be made and they must be based on accurate information. There needs to be strict controls on spending to be certain that anything that is not specifically needed for the fulfillment of the objectives of the nonprofit organization is jettisoned. The nonprofit needs to be very leery of debt and pay bills promptly. Purchase order forms must be in place so that staff do not make unapproved purchases. Strict measures need to be in place to be certain overspending does not occur.

One of the surest ways to kill a nonprofit organization, is for a lack of fiscal responsibility. Not only may it cause the debt load to be too high to operate properly it can cause supporters to lose confidence in an organization. There needs to be a tight monetary policy otherwise, the nonprofit will run amok. This needs to be communicated to every employee and board member to ensure financial strength. The noblest intentions remain unattainable if proper financing is not put in place first.

At the beginning of each year do a report to show what you accomplished in the previous year. Set new goals for the forthcoming year and strategies as to how to achieve them. Keep focused on what is most important. Remember that the good is the enemy of the best. If old tasks are dragging you down and preventing you from reaching your objectives remove them. Items of secondary importance should be sacrificed to allow your focus to remain on primary objectives.

On an annual basis, a nonprofit should sit down with board members and management to look at the strengths of the organization, the weaknesses, the opportunities that lie before it and the threats it faces. This SWOT analysis is a common tool to help organizations succeed. It is a popular brainstorming session to conduct an honest look at what needs to be achieved to achieve the objectives of the organization. It makes everyone feel they are part of the team and that their input is valuable. The best people to analyze a nonprofit are those working within the organization, because they see firsthand the situation as it truly exists.

A strategic plan is crucial for long-term viability because it implements steps to overcome obstacles. It shapes the organization so that it can be streamlined to achieve specific objectives. It blends future thinking with a present course of action. It is more than just a long-range plan because it sets out steps to reach goals. Without this strategic plan the organization is at the mercy of every force of opposition that could potentially bring it down. All the board members and staff members are needed to help formulate this component for the viability and sustainability of the nonprofit organization. It needs to be a coherent well-thought-out strategy Brainstorming sessions will take clever ideas and make them even better.

A strategic plan is setting out the direction a nonprofit will head in. It includes setting goals and the course of action that will be taken to achieve those goals. It starts by giving an overview of the organization and an analysis. Data is gathered from a variety of sources so that intelligent decisions can be made. Threats to the organization are examined, to take evasive action to neutralize them. Costs are looked at and examined as to whether they are reasonable. A financial plan and the strategic plan are not the same thing. The financial plan sets out an operating budget and how to raise the money. The strategic plan is setting out the objectives and goals of the organization.

In a strategic planning session, an organization sets out its priorities and determines what to leave behind. Employees agree on what they can work on together. It results in decisions for the overall improvement of the organization. It is always the right time for an organization to align itself with agreed-upon objectives and strategies and how to achieve those objectives. Steps are laid out on how to achieve the objectives and time frames are set for goals to be fulfilled.

If an organization doesn't already have a vision and mission statement this is the time to do it. For example, the vision statement of a University may be, "To be, an international university, producing leaders and top employees in their fields." The objectives may be to recruit fine students with outstanding potential, fund various chairs and acquire top professors who are constantly being published. The strategy could be wider recruitment of students and hiring new professors while firing inept ones. A target may be raising the level of student satisfaction and grade point averages.

It is difficult to combine being a visionary and operating as a day-to-day manager. Visionaries are often planning new ventures and become frustrated with the myriad of minute details required for day-to-day operations. Good managers are on top of technicalities and immediate concerns. However, if a person is only concerned with short-term matters the nonprofit organization may fall into difficult times. The balance between immediate needs and long-term vision casting is needed for the continuation of an organization. If one person does not have both qualities, then two people are needed to fulfill each role. Nonprofit organizations need visionary leaders to remain viable.

This chapter has emphasized the importance of strategic planning. It should be accomplished at least once a year and a complete a strict operating budget. A nonprofit organization needs to have a visionary at the helm to set out goals and enthuse employees. Valuing the input from volunteers and employees will raise the morale and stimulate overall productivity. This needs to be put in place before acquiring donors and supporters. If this kind of enthusiasm and shared vision exists it will be communicated to potential donors. When they sense this kind of commitment and vision they will not only give but will remain long-term supporters of the nonprofit organization. Organizations succeed because of strategic planning, clear, concise goals and proper fiscal management.

Chapter 5. Unique Challenges that Face Nonprofits

If people are experiencing economic hardship and they are looking to save money one of the first things they jettison is giving to a nonprofit. With this challenge come unique opportunities for nonprofits. People are looking for value and if you can demonstrate the benefit of your organization you will win their allegiance. If a nonprofit is vigilant it can rise above the difficulties. This chapter will address the subject of how a nonprofit can rise above obstacles. Hardships can be viewed as unique challenges instead of obstacles.

Dr. Roshani Shay of the Hawaii Wellness Institute said, "*All other challenges pale in comparison to the need for funding to keep our doors open and accomplish our mission,*" Barbara Wetzler of the SPCA of Central Florida, Inc. concurred, "*We never lack for vision, ideas or enthusiasm. The challenge is always finding sufficient funds today to safeguard the agency's financial vitality while working toward a progressive and stable future.*" It is no longer enough to just simply have a Director of Development; Nonprofit organizations need expertise in marketing. Nonprofits often face government cutbacks in funding, and increasing competition for donor dollars. The way to compensate for these obstacles is a better presentation of the charity's objectives to a wider audience.

Referring to the National Center for Charitable Statistics there are twice as many charities as Not for Profit organizations, and one tenth of the overall number are foundations. Examples of large nonprofit organizations are hospitals, universities, human services, and museums. Small organizations consist of theaters, neighborhood organizations and churches. We have the private sector, the government sector and then the nonprofit or third sector. When the government fails to provide the necessary services for its citizens it falls on the nonprofit sector to do more. Government cutbacks affect nonprofit organizations compounding the problem. Ideally, nonprofits can become less dependent on government grants. This will require more applications to foundations, however, this can be a very difficult procedure to meet the exacting requirements. If the nonprofit organization can hone its ability to secure foundation money the payoffs can be significant.

Many nonprofit organizations can place their ideals above reality, with devastating consequences. It is wonderful to uphold the objectives of the organization but not to the detriment of the cash flow statement. I'm a firm advocate that what makes sense in the corporate world applies to the nonprofit sector. By that I mean sound business principles need to be used in nonprofit organizations, otherwise they will become defunct. To some degree if a nonprofit organization does not act like a for-profit business in terms of fiscal management, it will cease to exist.

I maintain that you should never enter an endeavor with a break-even attitude. If you do not consider that an enterprise is going to yield more revenues than what are being expended it is best to leave it on the shelf. This applies to attending conferences, presentations and special events, etc. If an activity is not going to yield tangible benefits to offset the expenditure, then it should be avoided. An example would be, if having a booth at certain conference is not going to result in more supporters to offset the cost and expense, then the conference should be avoided. Idealism is fine in theory, however at some point reality must click in.

When the economy worsens, generally the need for nonprofits increases. The reduction of revenues and an increased workload is a recipe for disaster. When the social safety net develops holes, nonprofits are needed to help pick up the pieces. The National Council of Nonprofits reports that almost 75% of nonprofits have revenues under $500,000 and more than a third revenue supporting the work of charitable nonprofits annually originates with governments. Smaller nonprofits may have an especially tough time during downturns in the economy.

In a past era churches conducted more social work than they generally do today. Then, the government began to take over social services and the church was superseded. Now, however, with fiscal cutbacks in the government, churches need to pick up where governments are failing. The church needs to help provide social services to support the poor and needy. This will be a monumental task because so much of people's income today is taken up with taxes and just getting by. People do not have as much disposable income and hence they do not give as much as they otherwise would.

One of the greatest challenges facing nonprofits today is attracting and retaining good talent. Nonprofits pay less in salaries than businesses do. However, if nonprofits are not able to pay what corresponding positions in for-profit corporations do there will be a downward spiral. The way to break free is to concentrate resources to pay wages that are on par. If people are overworked and underpaid loyalty to the cause will only carry people so far. Difficult as it may be nonprofits need to invest in attracting the best employees and developing strong leadership. Otherwise, it is doomed to continue to repeat failures and function ineffectively.

Another area where nonprofits fail to invest properly is in technology. This causes the nonprofit sector to be cumbersome and sluggish. If nonprofit organizations expect to operate efficiently, they must recognize the importance of investing in technology. Technology relieves some of the workload of already overburdened staff and causes an organization to be efficient. Leaders that fail to recognize the importance of technology will find staff overwhelmed and eventually on the brink of quitting. Technology is as important to nonprofit organizations as it is for businesses in the for-profit sector.

"All too often, nonprofit organizations pin their hopes and dreams for fundraising on one person—namely, the Development Director. It has to be a priority, and a shared responsibility, for the board, the executive director and the staff alike" (Linda Wood Senior Director, Leadership and Grant making The Evelyn and Walter Haas, Jr. Fund). A Joint Project of Compass Point and the Evelyn and Walter Haas, Jr. Fund entitled, Underdeveloped: A National Study of Challenges Facing Nonprofit Fundraising defined cultivation as, *"any activity that builds awareness and*

connection for donors/funders and prospective donors/funders with your organization, and increases your understanding of why someone might give to your organization." It goes on to state, *"Most people in the organization (across positions) act as ambassadors and engage in relationship building. Everyone promotes philanthropy and can articulate a case for giving."* The position of Director of Development often has a high turnover for many organizations. This can be counteracted if all members on staff take an active role in developing funds.

Compass Point surveyed more than 2,700 executive directors and development directors. When a Director of Development comes open often is not filled for at least six months. Many Development Directors become discouraged and expect they will leave their job within two years. Many are not sure they will stay in their field. Nonprofit organizations would do well to help these people receive the resources and help they need to do their job effectively. This element of discouragement needs to be addressed for a nonprofit to break the cycle. A team approach is needed to donor development otherwise, the director feels overwhelmed.

It is very important for a nonprofit organization to realize that cultivation of relationships is the goal, not reaching financial targets. Until an organization sees that it is about building trust and developing long term friendships the funding of an organization will spike and plummet repeatedly. However, if there is an emphasis on slowly building a relationship with the donors, the income will steadily incline. The donor must be put ahead of the gift. If there is fair and effective communication most likely the donor will continue for many years to come. If the donor senses the organization is only concerned with the gift they will soon lose interest in giving support.

The Compass Point survey also revealed, *"Twenty-seven percent (27%) of executives leading organizations with operating budgets of $1 million or less reported being "very satisfied" with their development director's performance, compared to 41% of* *executives leading nonprofits of $10 million or more.*" One of the main reasons for this satisfaction is the director of development does not have the experience necessary. This is a very difficult, demanding role and proper training is needed if a person is expected to perform well. Tension can begin to mount within the nonprofit if there is a disconnect between the Executive Director and the Director of Development.

To combat the Director of Development turnover all the directors need to be involved in donor acquisition. Everyone should be able to present the mission of the organization and a case for supporting the organization. There needs to be a well thought out fund development strategy. Sufficient resources need to be allocated for this department as well as proper training. The necessary technology and support staff are needed, too. Investment in this department may yield good dividends. If it is neglected an executive director should not expect stellar results.

Obtaining revenue can be regarded as a unique challenge instead of an obstacle. A pilot looks at the windsock to see which way the wind is blowing. To the uninitiated one would expect he will go in the direction of the wind. Instead he points the nose of the plane into it to lift off. The shape of the wings and fuselage are such they create an updraft and like a mighty bird of prey with pinions and feathers angled perfectly the plane takes off. Similarly, the director of a nonprofit must look at obstacles as opportunities and see the challenges as an opportunity to present a case for giving. The nonprofit must show to the donor or supporter they are meeting a need in society that few others can fill. If the donor does not give or invest the problem will persist in society. Communicate the problem and show how the donor can solve it with a gift. This is flying into the wind and rising to meet the challenge.

The director of development for the nonprofit must tactfully present a case for giving. He or she must be conversant with the mission of the organization and can effectively communicate it. In so doing, the donor identifies with the need and rises to meet the challenge of solving the problem. Of course, the director must identify donors whose previous giving habits indicate they are concerned with the mission of the agency. For example, if the person loves animals they may very well be a potential donor to the local SPCA. The need must be seen and felt for the donor to be touched by the need. If they can feel the need they will be moved to get on board. One of the direct benefits to the donor is the feeling of gratification and knowing they have helped other people.

People love to hear a story. Many children were raised by parents who tucked them in at night with a bedtime story. Since the dawn of time groups of homo-sapiens sat around campfires telling stories. Oral tradition was the way to record history. Generally, oral tradition included storytelling. Write the story of your nonprofit and tell it repeatedly until people are very familiar with the mission of the organization you represent. Talk about how the organization is helping to change lives and how serious it would be if it ceased to operate. Use word pictures and give a clear description of the need and how the gift will make a tremendous difference.

Here is an introduction from a fundraising letter mailed by Covenant House and is offered as an example by Alan Sharpe: *"She stood on the curb looking scared and lonely in a skimpy halter top and bright red lipstick. It was two in the morning. A chilly breeze whipped up in the street and seemed to make her shiver. She was a child . . . just a child. We pulled our Covenant House van up to the curb and rolled down the window . . . ."* What a moving story that draws the reader into the sad world of child prostitution. Such a story is certain to touch the hearts of people. Few could ignore such a crucial plea.

"Every year, 5.8 million children die from hunger related causes. Every day that's 16,000 young lives lost forever. At Feed the Children, we work to put an end to world hunger...." This introduction certainly has a shocking effect, and the numbers are astounding. Every nonprofit organization needs to effectively present their case for support.

We were frozen with shock, amazement, and fear all at the same time... It had been a long and hard journey through Sudan, and at the end of it we were met by the frail, gaunt and starving bodies of children, teenagers, and adults all rushing towards us. Protruding rib cages and depressed stomachs. Legs as frail and thin as matchsticks. It was the most shocking sight we had ever seen. But with this sight came their smiles, their laughter, their cries of joy, and their warm embraces. Tears were shed on all our shoulders as we were hugged and thanked by many different people. And suddenly, we all realized how much what we were doing meant to all these people!"

Using stories and drawing people into the scene will make a connection between the supporters and the need.

Sumac is a complete, integrated software solution for nonprofits used to personalize and distribute electronic and paper communication, easily and cost-effectively. See sumac.com for more information. Draw the potential donor in with a story from real life. Give a suggested amount and be certain to personalize the letter. Show how they're giving can meet a very specific need.

A nonprofit organization can gain access to a list of foundations that have given to similar organizations in the past. It is very important that research is conducted on the Foundation to see the specific criteria they are looking for. Generally, a letter of introduction is sent and if the Foundation is interested they often have their own specific list of questions. They typically will want to have audited financial statements and may or may not require further follow-up for them to make their decision regarding giving. It is quite difficult and time-consuming and Foundations only give to organizations that specifically fall within the confines of their objectives. For example, if the Foundation is set up to help orphanages it may or may not give to establish schools. The two are not necessarily mutually exclusive, but Foundations have come to recognize they cannot help every charity that comes along. Therefore, it is so important for the director of a nonprofit to conduct research to see whether the donor is a good match for the nonprofit organization.

At the end of the day one of the most effective ways to raise money is to note those who have given significant amounts in the past. The director calls upon these individuals and quite possibly they will give more if they are asked. So, at this juncture, the director lays out the needs of the organization and asks for a significant amount that will allow the organization to meet their fundraising target. These people are already well versed with the operations of the organization and are more apt to give than someone who is being introduced to the nonprofit for the first time. Quite often people do not give more because they have not been asked to do so. They may be very willing to help in a larger way if they know of specific needs and there is a specific amount that is asked for.

The challenges that face nonprofits especially in times of fiscal restraint are mountainous. However, these mountains can be climbed and overcome if a proper strategy is put in place. This requires clearly stating the mission of the nonprofit and identifying donors that are a good fit for the organization. The directors of nonprofits need to remain optimistic and not lose sight of their goal. They are bound to meet obstacles, but they can be overcome. Clear strategies and a team approach will go a long way toward achieving financial sustainability. Nonprofit organizations need to remind themselves of why they are in operation and inspire themselves to keep pressing onward.

Chapter 6. Personnel Problems

Many nonprofit organizations are dependent upon volunteers. It has been my experience they can gain a sense of entitlement and be very difficult to manage. They feel because they are not on the payroll they do not need to follow specific instructions. Sometimes they can be quite undependable because they think they are already being very generous with their time. If something comes up they may not fulfill their obligation because they're tired or generally don't feel rewarded enough. It's important not to expect too much of volunteers. It would be better to lessen the responsibility placed on them and increase the number of paid staff if possible to not burn out the few eager ones.

The director of the nonprofit relying on volunteers needs to be firm but understanding in his or her expectations of volunteers. Generally, it's best to have a strict set of criteria before accepting a volunteer into a position of responsibility. The nonprofit organization needs to have a very clear application form and ask the person to sign an agreement. Volunteers can do a lot of harm to your organization if they are not in keeping with the standards that you set.

On a quarterly basis have a job review for employees. This is a good tool to ensure employees do not become distrustful or disgruntled. Allow it to be a safe environment where they feel secure in expressing how they are thinking. Here is an example of a Job Review from the The Catholic University of America, 620 Michigan Ave., N.E. Washington, DC.

INITIAL   REVIEW   PERIOD   PERFORMANCE EVALUATION

Employee Name: _____

Job Title: _____

Department: _____

Nonprofit Issues and Management

Hire Date: _____

Evaluation Period: _____

Date of Evaluation: _____

Evaluator Name: _____

INSTRUCTIONS

Read the description for each performance category. Check the appropriate rating. Provide any relevant comments for the boxes below. Additional room is provided below and if necessary accompanying sheets of paper can be included. Ratings are to be based upon your direct observations including feedback from reliable sources. Complete the final section indicating strengths and goals. Sign and date the Performance Evaluation. This is a two-way evaluation meaning the same sheets will be completed by the supervisor. Your self evaluation compared with the supervisor's evaluation of you will help him to determine if there is a communication problem, misunderstandings or misconceptions. A meeting will be scheduled with your supervisor to discuss this evaluation and provide an opportunity for you to express yourself verbally in addition to this written form.

PERFORMANCE RATINGS

OUTSTANDING: Performance is consistently and substantially above requirements in all areas; consistently exceptional performance over evaluation period. Few employees will receive this rating.

EXCEEDS REQUIREMENTS: Performance is clearly above requirements. Performance exceeds expectations of supervisor and requirements of job description. Normally few new employees will receive this rating.

Jeff Lutes

MEETS REQUIREMENTS: Performance is consistently good. This is the usual level of performance for most new hires. It is competent and effective performance relative to experience in the position.

NEEDS IMPROVEMENT: Performance does not fully meet requirements.

UNSATISFACTORY: Performance is unsatisfactory in critical areas.

	Out-stand-ing	Ex-ceeds Requi re-ments	Meets Requi re-ments	Needs impro ve-ment	Unsa tis-facto ry
Quality: Produces thorough, accurate and consistent work. Applies good judgment.					
Quantity: Produces required amount of work. Consistently completes fair share of the workload.					
Job Knowledge: Understands the overall job function and					

responsibilities as well as specific tasks. Has sufficient knowledge to perform job. Applies the concepts and skills. Knows and follows standard practices and departmental practices and procedures.					
Relationships: Cooperates with coworkers, supervisors, and others. Supports team effort and contributes to departmental goals. Is always courteous and acts in a professional manner. Acts respectfully toward others.					
Organization: Manages time effectively to plan and complete work. Sets and revises priorities as appropriate (with guidance as necessary from supervisor.)					
Initiative: Works independently. Performs appropriate					

tasks without being told. Suggests and develops procedures to make tasks easier and results more effective. Seeks increased assignment and responsibilities.					
Timeframe: Turnaround time consistently meets expectations. Completes tasks in a timely manner.					
Flexibility: Accepts new methods and changes. Works well under tight time constraints. Adapts willingly to changing priorities. Modify schedule to meet work demands.					
Dependability: Meets deadlines. Willing to work overtime when necessary. Demonstrates effective follow-through on short and long-term tasks.					

Professionalis m: Respectful and courteous both to clients and coworkers. Maintains a calm demeanor and demonstrates accountability.					
Communicatio n: Communicates effectively with supervisor, coworkers and clients. Listens well to instructions. Provides timely updates as appropriate. Maintains confidentiality. Asks appropriate questions when uncertain. clearly and effectively conveys information, demonstrates effective verbal and written communication skills, negotiates effectively.					
Problem-Solving: Identifies problems, enables others in seeking solutions, conducts appropriate analyses, searches for best					

solutions and responds quickly to new challenges.					
Strategic Planning and Organizing: Understands the overall picture and aligns priorities with broader goals, measures outcomes, uses feedback to redirect as needed, evaluates alternatives, solutions oriented, seeks alternatives and; can see connections within complex issues.					
Quality: High quality performance and takes initiative to make improvements.					
Attendance/Pu nctuality: Maintains satisfactory attendance. Arrives and departs as scheduled. Schedules days off in accordance with policy. Adheres to time allotted for lunch and break periods.					

Nonprofit Issues and Management

Strengths

1.)

2.)

3.)

Areas for improvement:

1.)

2.)

3.)

Reflections, explanations, and further comments:

Suggestions for the supervisor's improvement:

Employee's Signature:

Supervisor's Signature:

_____ Retain employee

_____ Discharge employee

_____ Extend Review

Here is the Employee Handbook that I use to settle problems before they arise.

SAMPLE EMPLOYEE HANDBOOK

My Commitment to You

Thank you for being a part of this ministry. You are valued as a person and respected. Your personal commitment to excellence will help this ministry advance the Gospel of Jesus Christ. My desire is that everyday will be a joy and a delight for you to come to work. If at any time, you would like to discuss anything pertaining to your working conditions you will find I have an empathetic ear. I am sure with free-flowing communication we can resolve issues, often solving them before they become a problem. I will work hard for you to ensure that always you have a safe, rewarding, fulfilling, personally enriching environment. If anyone or anything affects those standards I want to be the first to know.

Dr. Jeff Lutes - pres.

Personal Communications

Personal calls should be limited to no longer than five minutes in duration and no more than two calls per day. Staff should note that the phone is for ministry purposes and that business calls take precedence over personal calls. If it is necessary to make a personal call during office hours, the employee is asked to use his or her personal cell phone so as to leave the office line open. The same principle applies in that one or two personal cell phone calls per day is reasonable. Friends, and family members are welcome to come by the office for a visit for a reasonable length of time and a reasonable number of visits, i.e. once per week for no more than a half hour.

Equipment Usage

Equipment and tools belonging to the ministry are for company use only, i.e. microphones, sound equipment, computers.

Personal Emails and Web Surfing

THERE IS TO BE NO OUTSIDE WEB/INTERNET SURFING AND ANSWERING OF PERSONAL EMAILS at work on Office, Broadcast or Logger Computers.

Appearance, Cleanliness, Organization, Safety, Privacy, etc.

The offices, reception area and board room should be kept neat, with papers, files and books kept in desks, cabinets or on bookshelves. Dishes, cups and water glasses are to be cleaned or disposed of the day they are used. They must not be left lying around. It is unsanitary and unsightly. Please keep the office clean always. Personal items such as clothing are not to be left at the office overnight. Office work areas, desktops, et al are to be cleared off at the end of each day.

All papers are to be filed alphabetically for quick access. Invoices, letters, bills, etc. are to be filed or addressed at least one half hour before concluding the work day so they are not left lying around. Important financial information may potentially be left for people to see. Donors have the right to keep their gifts private. Out of practicality, during the work day said financial papers and other correspondence can be out on a desk top. We must be aware of confidentiality issues. Most certainly we would not want checks for deposit left out with courier drivers, mail carriers, and the public coming and going. There may be people who come in after hours. Each employee is expected to take his or her trash on a weekly basis.

The first impression when people come in the door is the operation is neat and orderly. There should be no cords left lying around for people to trip on. In winter, all steps are to be cleared of snow and ice. Salt is to be used to ensure walkways are not slippery. When people come in the door floor mats are to be laid out flat on the floor. Ensure that all tools are hung up immediately after they are used. All mic cables, electric cables, etc. are to be put away when not in use under their labels according to tip or connector type. No computer is to be sitting on the floor in case of flooding. Computers are to be on a stand up off the floor. Computers sitting on the floor are more likely to suck in damaging dust. All equipment is to be put away when not in use to prevent theft or damage.

Dress Code

The best way to describe our dress code would be "appropriate". Our standard dress code is "Business" or "Business Casual". If you are invited to speak in a Church setting, it is expected that you wear a tie and or suit jacket or for a lady, equally, appropriate attire. Dress for other engagements should be based on the type of meeting or conference.

Office Hours, Lunch and Break Times

Office hours are subject to the discretion of the President. However, it is expected that a work day would consist of eight hours with a lunch hour and standard breaks. The lunch break should be as close to the noon hour as possible for one half hour. A fifteen-minute break can be taken in the morning and one in the afternoon. It is encouraged that the lunch break be off premises but not the fifteen minute breaks. Exceptions can be made for employees who would like to combine their two fifteen minute breaks to form an hour at lunch time. If hours are being worked other than the standard 9-to-5 then it is the employee's responsibility to keep a timesheet. This will serve as verification for overtime and must be signed by the president.

It is also recognized that at times employees are required to meet with clients, board members, etc. in the carrying out of business. Some of these meetings may take place out of the office. These meetings are counted as office hours.

Sickness and Personal Time

If sickness interrupts one's ability to perform the duties required, you must immediately contact other Station Personnel and the President to ensure duties are covered. You must report if you are sick and unable to come to work as early as possible, directly by phone. Arrangements for a suitable replacement are needed.

The ministry does not have healthcare coverage and if an employee becomes disabled or is unable to work they must apply to the government for benefits. The ministry does not have resources allocated to continue paying a person if they are unable to carry out their duties.

We realize there are occasional times when you need to be away from work for personal reasons, illness or appointments with doctors. Each full-time person will be given a reasonable number of sick days. More than six sick days per year requires other arrangements. Time used above the allowable six days per year will be unpaid or taken as vacation days. A sick day must be legitimate and the employer retains the right to ask for a doctor's certificate to prove the validity of a sick day. The year runs from the anniversary date of an employee starting to the end of twelve months. Sick days are not additional holiday time. For example, a person cannot use up their holidays and then pretend they are sick to get extra time off.

The ministry will be sensitive should an employee find himself or herself facing a personal crisis. The employee is encouraged to receive counselling if necessary at a cost not paid by the ministry. Time will be made available for a person to work through a crisis or personal problem, provided it is brought to the employer's attention. We want to be sensitive to personal needs. However, this kindness cannot be abused. If psychological reasons or other health related issues are preventing an employee from carrying out work responsibilities the employer needs to be notified well in advance. Lying and covering up information is not ethical. Emotional imbalances must be verified by a registered psychologist. Issues outside the work environment need to be addressed as well as those immediately related. Personal or mental health days need to be approved in advance by the president.

Maternity, Parental and Adoptive Leave

Maternity/Parental/Adoptive and other government supported Leave shall conform to the provisions of the Employment Standards Act. The full period of the Leave is granted without pay. The ministry will issue a Record of Employment on commencement of Leave which allows the employees to make claim for Employment Insurance Benefits. When the employee returns to work, employment is guaranteed in a similar position at the same salary level. During the full period of Leave, vacation and sick leave shall continue to accumulate.

Professional Development

At the discretion of the President, employees may be able to attend conferences, courses, seminars and meetings, identified through annual work plans and performance reviews, which may be beneficial to the employee's professional development. If these opportunities are directly related to the employee's position, or are suggested by the President, then the ministry will cover some or all of the cost associated, i.e. registration, course materials, some travel and hotel expenses. An application must be made to the president directly for time to attend a conference or an educational event.

If the ministry has agreed to pay for a course the fees will be paid on evidence of successful completion. If the ministry sponsors a course (or courses) and the employee departs ministry within a year of completion, the course fees will become repayable in full.

Confidential Information and Intellectual Property

Confidential Information

From time to time, employees of the ministry may come into contact with confidential information, including but not limited to information about the ministry's members, suppliers, finances and business plans. Employees are required to keep any such matters that may be disclosed to them or learned by them confidential. The Station Manual is considered highly confidential and contains intellectual property belonging to the ministry. It is expected that should an employee no longer be with the ministry all copies in his or her possession be destroyed. This includes software, passwords, etc. All access to ministry computers would have to desist. This is especially important in relation to the Financial Manual. At no time is this to be circulated outside of the office. It is highly confidential.

Furthermore, any such confidential information, obtained through employment with the ministry, must not be used by an employee for personal gain or to further an outside enterprise or company. All information pertaining to setting up a station and its operation is considered intellectual property and may not be used for one's personal benefit or the benefit of another organization. This applies to board members as well.

If a former employee or board member takes knowledge gained from the ministry to use to start a competing radio station or to work for a station in any of the markets where we have licenses, without personal permission from the president, this will be considered a breach and legal action if necessary will be taken.

Intellectual Property

Any intellectual property including but not limited to trademarks, copyrights and patents, and any work created by an employee in the course of employment at the ministry shall be the property of the ministry and the employee is deemed to have waived all rights in favour of the ministry. Work, for the purpose of this policy refers to written, creative or media work. All source material used in presentation or written documents must be acknowledged.

IT Information Storage and Security

All employees are expected to have their work backed up on an external hard drive each day. This includes work they do for the ministry on a personal computer. Any storage devices (CD's,

USB's, and offsite storage services such as cloud computing or virtual servers) used by employees at the ministry, located at the ministry's address, acknowledge that these devices and their contents are the property of the ministry. Furthermore, it should be understood by employees, that company equipment should be used for company business only during normal working hours. Downloading of personal materials on company equipment can be harmful to said equipment and should not be done.

Computer printouts are not for public use or distribution. All printouts are to remain as ministry property and are not to be given out to individuals for personal business. Printouts of relevant material may be made for official committees, ministry officers and department leaders for the fulfilment of their duties. Confidential records such as promissory notes and giving records will not be distributed to any individual. Mailing lists or telephone directories may be made available to leaders who need them to fulfil their ministries. Any personal copies of manuals are to be destroyed should a person no longer be with the ministry.

Disposal of Items with Value

These are items which individually have a sale value of $50.00 or more. Items valued at up to $250.00 which have become obsolete, may be disposed of by the Administrator. Items valued at over $250.00 must have the approval of the Director or Treasurer for disposal.

Health and Safety

The ministry, along with its employees, must take reasonable precautions to ensure that the workplace is safe. The ministry complies with all requirements for creating a healthy and safe workplace in accordance with the Occupational Health and Safety Act. Employees who have health and safety concerns or identify potential hazards should contact the president. No employee shall create an opportunity for a safety hazard for himself, herself or any other employee either directly or indirectly. Carelessness is unacceptable. Alcohol consumption or illegal drug use is not permitted during work hours on the premises. If alcohol or drug use becomes an issue, i.e. affecting job performance, judgment then corrective measures must be taken by the employee. If the person using drugs or alcohol does not admit the problem or take remedial action, then measure will be taken by the employer to ensure the problem does not continue. This could be as serious as immediate dismissal. Him and

Pets

The offices of the ministry are a place of business, and as such, pets are not welcome during normal working hours. Staff and visitors with seeing-eye dogs are the exception.

Harassment

The ministry wants to provide a harassment-free environment for its employees and volunteers. Mutual respect, along with cooperation and understanding, must be the basis of interaction between members and staff. The ministry will neither tolerate nor condone behaviour that is likely to undermine the dignity or self-esteem of an individual, or create an intimidating, hostile or offensive environment. Sexual harassment is any unwanted attention of a sexual nature such as remarks about appearance or personal life, offensive written or visual actions like graffiti or degrading pictures, physical contact of any kind, or sexual demands.

There are several forms of harassment but all can be defined as any unwelcome action by any person, whether verbal or physical, on a single or repeated basis, which humiliates insults or degrades. "Unwelcome", for the purposes of this policy, refers to any action which the harasser knows or ought to reasonably know is not desired by the victim of the harassment. Specifically, racial harassment is defined as any unwelcome comments, racist statements, slurs, jokes, graffiti or literature or pictures and posters which may intentionally or unintentionally offend another person.

Workplace Violence

Workplace violence can be defined as a threat or an act of aggression resulting in physical or psychological damage, pain or injury to a worker, which arises during work. Further to the definition of violence, is the definition of abuse. Abuse can be verbal, psychological or sexual in nature. Verbal abuse is the use of unwelcome, embarrassing, offensive, threatening or degrading comments. Psychological abuse is an act which provokes fear or diminishes a person's dignity or self-esteem. Finally, sexual abuse is any unwelcome verbal or physical advance or sexually explicit statement.

The ministry has a zero-tolerance limit with regards to harassment and violence. Employees or volunteers engaging in either harassing or violent activities will be subject to discipline, which may include termination of employment, removal from Boards or committees and possibly criminal charges. Loose sexual talk, innuendos and otherwise insinuations is not becoming of a Christian worker. Ministry personnel are to be examples of Christian behaviour always. Failure to comply must be reported immediately.

Dispute Resolution

Regrettably, conflict can occur in any working environment. In an effort to resolve conflict in an expedient, yet fair manner, the ministry recommends the following process for conflict or dispute resolution.

Ø Speak to the person you are having the dispute with. Many times, disputes arise due to misunderstandings and miscommunications.

Ø If speaking to the individual does not work, speak to the president or his designate. The president will arrange a meeting between those involved in the dispute, to determine a resolution.

Ø If the president is unable to resolve a workplace dispute, the parties may be referred to mediation by an outside third party. The resolution of the mediator is binding on both parties of the dispute.

Job Evaluations

Job evaluations are quarterly. If poor performance is not rectified it can result in termination.

Conduct and Discipline Policies

Failure to report issues may result in termination of employment. If an employee is found to be in breach of any agreements with the ministry immediate termination of employment will occur. If a matter is reported early, then tolerance may be shown. This is provided a period of discipline is accepted. Behaviour problems that are a discredit to the ministry will not be condoned. The employer retains the right to place an employee on probation but is not limited to provide a period of probation.

Respect of Authority

Nonprofit Issues and Management

Filing grievances with supervisors and/or co-workers must be done so in writing to the president. Conduct at all time is to be respectful toward the president and his designates. Authority is to be respected. If conduct is found unsatisfactory action will be taken. It is understood that you will not take these grievances to outside persons, without first presenting them in writing to the president. They are to be handled within the office.

Policies for Promotion or Demotion

This is at the discretion of the president and is related to the quarterly reviews.

Attendance Issues

Being late for work and missing time is unacceptable. The employer can require proof that an employee is arriving for work on time, at the office when not supervised and not leaving before the understood time. If the employee cannot produce evidence that he or she has been at his or her workstation during the expected hours of operation then the employer reserves the right to deduct pay. Exceptions are made for storms, road work, etc. or anything that would otherwise be considered a logical reason for not being at work. The employer does not expect an employee to travel to and from the office when weather conditions create a driving hazard. In the event of forecasted storms it is expected that an employee arrives at work if the present driving conditions are reasonable. If during the workday, a storm ensues good judgment would mean leaving the office to travel home in a safe manner.

Jury Duty

If you are called for jury duty, this time will not count as vacation or discretionary time-off and will include full pay up to a maximum of 10 working days.

Media

All media matters are to be handled exclusively by the president. If media contact the station for interviews or answers to questions these are to be referred to the president.

Paid Holidays

We recognize the following holidays for full time employees with full salary:

- New Year's Day

- Victoria Day

- Good Friday

- Canada Day - July 1

- The First Monday of August

- Labour Day

- Thanksgiving Day

- Remembrance Day

- Christmas Day

- Boxing Day

When a statutory holiday occurs during an employee's vacation, the vacation will be extended by one extra day.

Leave of Absence

A leave of absence without pay, necessitated by circumstances beyond your control may be granted. This is at the discretion of the President. A reason in writing will be presented for consideration.

Vacation Plan and Pay

Vacation with pay for full time staff will be provided during the time the person is off. Vacation pay is not added to each check throughout the year. The person receives their pay while they are on vacation. A request for vacation time must be coordinated with the president one full month in advance. If the vacation period requested is the same as that of another person on staff then a suitable alternative period will have to be chosen. This written request will be obliged as a suitable, trained replacement is in place to cover the person's responsibilities. This can take up to three months. If after one year there are remaining vacation days they can be carried over to a successive year. One full year of employment must be completed before any vacation days can be used.

Vacation Schedule:

1-4 years 2 weeks/year

5-9 years 3 weeks/year

10+ years 4 weeks/year

Funeral Time

In the event of death in the immediate family, you will be allowed a leave of five days immediately following the death with full salary being paid. Further time-off or time-off for the death of any other relative or friend must be taken either as unpaid, vacation days, or sick time. Members of the immediate family includes: spouse, father, mother, sister, brother, son, daughter, grandparent, any in-law, and relative with whom you reside. A step-relative must be someone who lives with you to constitute paid bereavement time.

Termination of Employment

In the event of the employer terminating your employment, employment law will be used, i.e. two-week notice will be provided. If the employee is terminated his or her employment correspondingly two-week notice must be given to the employer.

The board is involved in the overall ministry to ensure the goals and objectives are being accomplished. Staffing issues are the responsibility of the president and or his designate and not that of the board. The board is a volunteer group and are not held responsible for employee situations. The employee reports to the president and not the board. The board is not involved in employee matters.

Generally, verbal warnings will be given for incompetence, repeated mistakes or unsatisfactory work. If necessary changes and improvements are not implemented next email messages will be sent stipulating matters more definitely. Thirdly, a notice of termination will be given. It is anticipated the matters will have long since been resolved before stage three occurs. By stage two, namely emails documenting unsatisfactory work or behaviour will be sent verifying that an employee is placed on probation.

Dismissal will occur after dialogue and other methods have not yielded satisfactory results.

Grievances are to be brought directly to the attention of the president. If verbal communications do not solve an issue the employee is encouraged to put his or her concerns in writing. Should an employee resign, a Letter of Resignation should be written giving the president a two week notice and stating the reason for resignation and the final date of services.

Retirement

The normal staff age for retirement is age 65. A staff member may continue employment, full time or part time after that age if he/she submits a written request for an extension, of up to six months that is recommended by the President and approved by the Board of Directors. The written request for "extended employment", addressed to the President, must be submitted three months prior to the month of his/her 65th birthday.

Job Description

The president reserves the right to revise a job description at any given time. The employee is expected to accommodate changes in work circumstances. Ministries, and companies need to be continually changing and developing to address economic conditions, competition, changes in technology, etc. In order to stay financially viable and effective It may be necessary to update, modify or otherwise change a person's job. Tasks not immediately described in an initial job description are expected to be attended to. Employees need to be willing to accommodate the circumstances and be flexible.

Personnel Files and Employment Records

Employment records for each staff member will be confidential. Records must be kept for 7 years. A personnel file, on all employees, shall be maintained in the President's office. The file will contain:

- Resume and references

- Employee's Withholding Allowance Certificate

- Agreement of Employment/Job Covenant

- Job Description (revised and original)

- Assigned Tasks

- Regular Weekly Worksheet Timetable

- Employee History (salary, attendance, etc.)

- Annual and quarterly Evaluations

- Five Year Ministry Goals and Evaluations

- Vacation and Absentee Record

- Signed statement by Administrator at time of hiring

A Personnel file shall be maintained by the Administrator for current information regarding:

- Leave and attendance applications

- Record of attendance

- Leave summaries

Salary Payments

All employees are paid once per week on Friday. The pay is transferred on Thursday only to ensure it is received by Friday. When that pay falls on a holiday or weekend, you will be paid on the day proceeding. If a commission or remuneration applies, it will be payable after the Station receives payment from the sale. All salaries paid will have the necessary source deductions remitted on the employee's behalf including income tax, CPP and UIC deductions including the employer's' share. A pay stub can be requested each pay period or for a term.

Payroll Deductions and Personal Record Changes

The law requires deductions for income tax for salaried employees. A statement highlighting each deduction will be given at the end of each year. A statement will also be issued if there are changes in an employee's deductions. It is the responsibility of the employee to inform the ministry of any change in address, marital status, telephone number, and number of dependents.

Employee Group Benefits Program

To be discussed.

Compensation

Employee's salaries shall be reviewed before December 31 of each year by the president, and recommendations for salary will be forwarded to the Board of Directors.

Job Performance Review

The Employee job performance will be reviewed quarterly and recommendations as to whether to retain an employee will be made by the president.

Raises, Overtime and Severance Pay

An employee cannot expect a raise if they are not bringing more to the organization. The employer is under no obligation to pay over time as this is a salaried position and not an hourly one. One week's severance pay for every full year worked is paid after termination for employees who have worked over six years.

Layoffs and Job Restructuring

If finances are not available the employer has the right to layoff an employee until further notice. From time to time it may be necessary to restructure jobs. The employee has a right to reapply. However, there is no obligation to bring the person back on staff. If a person's position is terminated they are to return all ministry property and turn in all keys belonging to the ministry. They are to have no further access to the building or computers. All passwords are to be deleted.

Workers Compensation Insurance

The ministry does not carry Workers Compensation Insurance for on the job injury. In the case of less than five employees the employer is not required to have a separate policy as this would be paid / provided by the government. We have less than five employees.

Travel-related Expenses

These must be approved before hand and all receipts must be retained. The ministry will approve .55 cents for the first 5,000 kms. per year and.45 cents per kilometre after that for use of a personal automobile to attend to a ministry function.

Life-style and Morality and Code of Ethical Fundraising Statements

These are to be signed and kept on record. This applies to time both during normal working hours and after hours.

Disclaimer and Updates

This document can be updated at any time and will replace previous editions. The employee is expected to sign new copies, each time.

Acknowledgement

I hereby acknowledge that I have read and understand this Employee Handbook and further acknowledge acceptance of all its terms and conditions.

Jeff Lutes

      In witness, whereof the parties have duly executed this Employee Handbook agreement this _____ day of _____ 201__.

      Staff Member

Confidentiality Agreement

      Agreement made as of _____(date) between (name of Nonprofit). and any of its subsidiaries, and _____(name of employee, volunteer or board member.)

      Given that some information entrusted to employees and board members can be of a confidential nature and if misappropriated can do damage all persons connected to the organization are asked to sign this letter of confidentiality. Codes and passwords are provided to us by companies wishing to promote their music and programs. This privilege can be abused by the unlawful downloading of music and programming for personal use and or distribution which has the potential of affecting the revenues of broadcast ministries and artists. Our manual contains intellectual property gleaned from years of broadcasting that would be unfair to misappropriate.

      Further to this, those involved in the handling of receipting donors, issuing receipts, billing, etc. could potentially pass on information to third parties that may violate confidentiality. This document is meant to protect the ministry from any who would misappropriate financial information about the receipting practices and disbursement of funds for the operation of the ministry. Legitimate enquiries are to be directed to the ministry office for an appointment to view requested documents, i.e. audits, budgets, financial records, constitution. This document is binding even after resignation, dismissal, transfer, or otherwise no longer with the ministry. It is understood that any questions are to be directed to the president for permission to pass on to a third party anything that should it be misconstrued could create damage to the ministry.

Confidential information means in any form (print, digital, .wav, mpeg, etc.) not generally known to the public, disclosed to or acquired by the employee, volunteer or board member directly or indirectly from the employer or clients, churches or affiliates during the term of employment or service without limitation. The employee, volunteer or board member will not at any time use confidential information for any other purpose than the carrying out of his or her duties. Upon resignation, dismissal or completion of a term an employee, volunteer or board member will return all materials and property belonging to the ministry.

This shall be in accordance with the laws of this province and the Dominion of Canada. Failure to adhere to the intent of this agreement may result in remedial action. It is a serious offence to provide information to third parties or use information personally that may result in damage to the ministry. The employee, volunteer or board member agrees that no amendment to this document is binding without the express agreement of the board of directors and founder/president. The employee, volunteer or board member acknowledges that they have read this document in its entirety and that he or she understands it. Said person agrees to be bound by all the conditions set out in it.

Name of employee, volunteer or board member

_____

Please sign on the line above and return to

Rev. Dr. Jeff Lutes Founder/President

A 2013 Gallup Study showed only 13% of employees worldwide were engaged, whereas the clear majority of employees were either not engaged or actively disengaged in the workplace. This means that nearly 9/10 of all workers are either just going through the motions of their daily jobs or are actively looking for new job. The Predictive Index Lists five best practices organizations to maximize engagement and retain top talent. Starting with, design jobs with growth opportunities Predictive Index reminds us that people flourish and opportunities that support learning and development. Next, it is important for employers to monitor job satisfaction because if employees are satisfied they are less likely to leave. Thirdly, maximize employee embeddedness, meaning that the employer needs to help the employee connect with the organization fourthly, manage early interactions by providing clear and early communication about the values of the organization. Be certain there are frequent check-ins to keep the lines of communication flow. Lastly, develop great leaders by demonstrating a commitment to the team. If the employee connects with the manager there is a higher likelihood that person will stay with the organization for a long time.

Chapter 7. Leadership and Management Skills

A comprehensive knowledge of leadership and management skills are necessary for directing a nonprofit organization. Leadership skills are needed for the heads of nonprofits the same as they are for CEOs and presidents of for profit corporations. They set out the direction and objectives of the organization. Managers are expected to motivate personnel to achieve the objectives of the Corporation. It is one thing to establish goals and it is quite another to fulfill them and motivate others to help accomplish them. Often there is mistrust of leadership on the part of employees. It behooves the manager to build a sense of comradery amongst the employees of the company. When morale is low a corporation fails to meet its objectives. The task of managers is to inspire employees to pull together and help achieve the objectives as set out by the Leaders of the company.

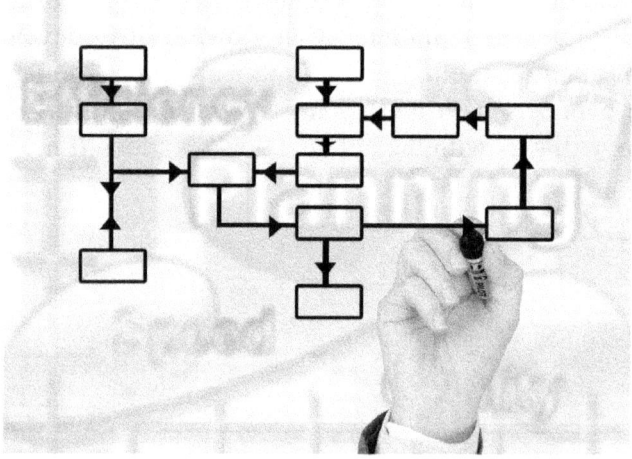

In a profit-based company quite often all decisions are made through the lens of how operations can be run more efficiently to produce more money. A company may be making lots of money however operational costs are still cut so that overall profits are driven even higher. This can reduce employee morale when they are expected to work harder with less. A nonprofit company generally has a different set of objectives and hence may be a more fulfilling place to work. If the objectives are to provide quality healthcare while cost-saving measures are important the personal satisfaction of the employee of the nonprofit Corporation may be high when they see patients recuperating.

Similarly, in an educational facility professors and even support staff will have a sense of satisfaction knowing their efforts are rewarded by helping students go on to achieve fulfilling careers. A wise personnel manager may schedule quarterly meetings for staff and teachers whereby students who graduated five years, ten years and even longer return to the institution to share how their studies particularly equipped them to succeed in their chosen professions. This will help build morale in an educational facility.

A leader sets out the objectives for his or her department and inspires others to feel like they are part of the team and their daily work is making a difference. If everyone sees how crucial their role is in a nonprofit, then there is a greater likelihood they will be productive. For example, if a custodian fails to mop the floor, take out trash and clean the offices potentially accidents can happen and people can become sick thus inhibiting them from accomplishing their tasks. A wise manager will even take the time to encourage support staff and other necessary personnel for the smooth operation of a company. A little praise can go a long way to fuel a person to give their best effort daily.

A wise manager is a good listener. He or she often has an open-door policy, meaning employees are welcome to bring their concerns at any time. In these discussions, it may be discovered ways to improve overall efficiency. Granted these meetings may need to be scheduled, however they are important for overall efficiency. When each person on staff feels valued and important there is a lower likelihood of staff turnover and low productivity. Financial remuneration is a motivator but not the best one. If people like their supervisor and their work environment they may even be willing to stay in the position when another company may try to offer a larger salary package.

Leaders need to be able to think strategically and set up a course of action for the organization. Great generals surmise their enemy's weaknesses and attack them at their point of greatest vulnerability. The strong leader of a nonprofit organization needs to set out the battle plan for the organization to take new ground. This is both in terms of the long-term vision and short-term step-by-step instructions. You must set out where you believe the organization can be for example in five years and what it will take to achieve those objectives. Every six months these plans need to be discussed thoroughly and to see if the organization is on track for achieving its goals.

Allow me to state at this juncture that the qualities of a good leader and manager are intertwined in this is discussion. They are two separate roles but quite often a manager must fulfill the role of leader because the organization is too small to have a specific person to fulfill this role in the organization or the leader does not fulfill his or her duties. It is good for a manager to have leadership qualities and to be able to fulfill this function. However, as organizations grow they need to have both a distinct leader in a specific position and separate managers. Good leaders are not necessarily good managers. Meaning they can vision cast and set out the strategy without being an organizational person to attend to a myriad of details. Managers need to be detail people who are certain that tasks are completed. Leaders may not always be good at interpersonal relationships because they are so singular in their focus. Managers must have good people skills.

Good leaders are organized and know how to immediately obtain the information they are looking for to solve problems. It's important for a leader to be clear and decisive in his or her actions. They need to be able to communicate their objectives clearly to be understood. A good leader can identify what is important and leave behind what is unnecessary. The leader of the organization must be a good role model and not allow himself or herself to get bogged down in a myriad of difficulties and details. It is important for this person to be able to keep a level head and to be in control of the situation always.

It's not enough to simply set out goals; there must be strategic steps to achieve them. In other words, the leader needs to have a plan of attack. A quarterback tells his team members where he wants them to be positioned when he throws the football. The hockey team captain sets the example for the team and shows the strategy to put the puck in the net. Similarly, the leader of the team for a nonprofit organization can inspire confidence, set a good example, and give clear directions. He or she needs to break down larger tasks into smaller ones for the people in his or her employ.

An effective leader always has a contingency plan and is ready to put it into action when necessary. This person is always thinking for five steps ahead and preparing for what could possibly go wrong. It is important to have backup plans so that everything doesn't run amok. When a crisis hits it's very important for the leader to remain calm so that his or her fellow team members can take confidence. The best way to avoid problems is to plan. A good leader is always one or two steps ahead and able to confidently lead and deflect problems. Plan for what could go wrong and hopefully it will never come to pass.

Risks are necessary for progress; however, they should be calculated to avoid surprises. Leaders often have a different psychological makeup and managers. By nature, they are risk takers where as managers may be more cautious. When something does go wrong, try to contain it immediately so that it does not worsen. Deal with issues quickly, before they come out, such as staff tensions, financial shortages, etc. A strong leader is someone who has developed analytical skills, and can survey problems and quickly extinguished them.

A leader must stay positive always; however, this is not implying a Pollyanna view of the world. The leader is optimistic without being overconfident. This kind of positivism will encourage confidence on the part of the employees. Some people see a problem for every solution. Quickly contain those who have a negative, critical attitude and do not allow this person to sour the entire group. Take their critiques seriously, however, disassemble the points in their argument that undo your vision for the organization. Don't allow the morale of the company or organization to be deflated by a few naysayers. Take these people aside individually and work to change their attitude otherwise it will be contagious. Do not allow them to control or manipulate a meeting. Show that you are in control always.

Keep a positive attitude by meditating and finding inner peace. Write out your thoughts and develop your strategies so that you can remain optimistic. Come to work each day with an optimistic outlook on life so that your enthusiasm transfers to the entire team. Set the tone of optimism and confidence so that the organization will grow, develop and achieve objectives. Negativity is the enemy and must be contained always. This is not to ignore problems or stave off the inevitable if difficulties are arising. It is simply saying that a positive attitude will empower people and give them a sense of victory.

One of the first steps to overcome a problem is to identify it. Begin to propose various solutions and choose the best course of action to overcome the difficulty. Give a careful analysis to not overlook critical matters. Work on solutions with your team and make it a team effort. Allow people to be part of the problem-solving process so they feel empowered and want to take part. Empower people and assign areas of responsibility so they are feel valued. Problems should not be looked upon as simply a set of difficulties rather as opportunities to prove the worthiness of the organization.

Time management is extremely important, so that the right priority is given to the most urgent tasks. Often lesser problems will meddle and prevent the overall objectives from ever being achieved. It is important to use time as efficiently as one uses money. It's always possible to make more money, but it's not possible to regain lost time. Time is a very precious commodity and it is limited for everyone. So, therefore it is so important to stay organized and use time efficiently. A good leader is someone who uses his or her time wisely. It is generally a very good use of time to have personal meetings with employees and to be certain they feel like they are being heard and understood. It is a very good use of time to build relationships with employees and fellow workers.

It is very tempting to procrastinate and put off important projects. What you can do today should not be put off until tomorrow or next week. Attack problems immediately as they arrive so they do not have the opportunity to compound. A good leader is decisive and when he decides, he or she sticks with it unless it's wrong. The leader does not waffle between decisions and options. Rather, he or she surveys the situation, makes a definite course of action, and follows the plan through to completion. Going back and forth is a terrible waste of time. It's important to be decisive and precise in one's actions otherwise valuable time and resources are lost.

A good leader is optimistic and self-motivated. If you are motivated it will inspire other people to get involved as well. A good leader is enthusiastic and filled with optimism. Positive thinking and a can-do mentality spread throughout the organization inspiring people in the company. A good leader never dithers or speaks negative, self doubting thoughts. Rather, he or she is inspired and presses on. If there are times of personal self doubt, then you should remove yourself from the situation so that you do not discourage others. At all times remain positive and optimistic about the future so the seeds of doubt are not given a chance to germinate in the nonprofit organization.

People skills are very important for the leader. He or she must be a very good listener and be tactful in their approach with employees. If the leader is abrasive and obnoxious people will soon lose confidence and not want to follow him or her. It is important to empower other people and express how much you value them. Rude behavior is always unprofessional in the office. Being kind and complementary will yield much better results than negativity and criticism. Always be uplifting and never be afraid to give a word of praise or commendation to an employee who has done a good job.

Be assertive without being overbearing. Be self-confident without being arrogant. Leaders who are selfish and always talking about themselves and will incur gossip and backbiting. It is important to be humble and to give recognition to employees for their good ideas. Don't take credit for what employees have done, because this will cause people to be disgruntled. Always give credit where credit is due and it's important to say please and thank you in the office. Treat people with respect and they will show you respect, quite often. There are always exceptions to the rule but people will look up to a manager or leader who is kind, respectful, courteous, and complementary.

Inspire and motivate the people who are around you by personal discipline and commitment to the cause. Be a conscientious person and understanding of those who are around you. It is difficult to inspire people when you are negative, belittling others with gossip and overall not a nice person. These may seem unimportant for being a leader. However, these common-sense rules are what makes a great leader. Employees want to be treated with dignity, respect and sensitivity always. Too often, employees are taken for granted and then the leader wonders why people are not effective in their jobs. People can feel demoralized and unenthused. When they are not appreciated, and respected their productivity and job satisfaction level decrease. It is very important to show personal interest in the people that you work with. If you show genuine care and are sensitive and thoughtful they often will go the extra mile.

Good managers have a degree of technical skill and great strengths in dealing with people. They need to be able to conceptualize, and communicate well. Human skills mean the ability to interact with employees and motivate them. Conceptual skills are the ability to understand problems and develop strategies. They need to be able to make sound business decisions guided by wisdom. Is often difficult to find these qualities in one person. However, each of them are necessary to fulfill the role of a manager. A good manager is someone who can control his or her emotions and deal well with the emotions of others. It is important that the emotions be kept in check in the nonprofit organization for it to function well. The manager oversees this important matter to make sure that things do not get out of hand.

Management and leadership are not interchangeable terms. A person can be a good leader without being a good manager and vice versa. A leader inspires and sets out the direction for a Corporation while a manager is someone who manages people. Not all visionary people have strong people skills. We move now, in our discussion from leadership to an examination of management. Managers are responsible for making sure things go well. Leaders may be very good at setting out the vision and inspiring people but very poor, for example at delegation because they try to do everything themselves. A good manager is someone who knows how to delegate. To have long-term success a nonprofit need to make sure it has good managers.

A good manager monitors the team and helps them to solve their own problems. A manager is someone who relates well with employees and builds strong interpersonal relationships. Good managers also have strong communication skills, and can relate to the people around them. Sometimes there could be jealousies and inter-office competition. A good manager is someone who knows how to quell these sorts of disagreements. Good managers also know how to pick the right person for the right job. They avoid trying to put a square peg in a round hole and they work hard to ensure that people have an elevated level of job satisfaction.

Meetings are important to ensure work is flowing and progressing nicely. It provides an opportunity for people to express themselves and feel valued as a team member. It's an opportunity to show that many heads are better than one, because people can politely critique ideas and then rebuild concepts to be better than before. This is done by gently examining an idea in a group setting. People can offer constructive criticism and it is at this point that it is especially important that managers have the skills to quell any dissatisfaction or hurt feelings. Otherwise, people become disinterested and avoid working together as a team. A manager must have great skill in being able to avoid conflicts that have the potential to cause everything to blow up. The manager is often delicately balancing personalities to make sure that people can be congenial with one another. This takes a tremendous amount of people skills and that is what allows the manager to succeed in his or her role.

A good manager is someone who can basically balance and create a good dynamic in the organization. It is important to be able to quell interoffice politics, jockeying for power and prestige and influence over others. The manager needs to establish themselves as the one in charge in the group without being overbearing. Otherwise, power struggles begin to develop and this can derail the organization from being effective. This is where vision casting comes in, because if everyone buys into the concept of what the overall mission is you can help people to put aside personal hurts and personal agendas.

Fixing a computer, for example is a matter of eliminating what the problem is not while focusing in on what most likely is the cause. The human mind is much more complex than a computer and people can change their feelings and thoughts in a moment without any real indication. Communication is the lifeblood to the nonprofit organization and there is no substitute for personal attention and individual meetings with people to make sure they are feeling valued and recognized. A manager is more than a technician with knowledge of how to do the job. They are someone who has strong people skills, is respected and congenial. Technician are often introverted and do not make good managers. A manager must be amicable and able to relate to how people are feeling about their job.

A manager has many skills such as delegation, inspiring others, time management, etc. They can make clear decisions based on facts and take the time to gather the information necessary to develop the best possible course of action. Planning and coordinating are highly important to make sure that a nonprofit can achieve its objectives. A manager must be extremely organized and can set out the necessary steps for the nonprofit to achieve its objectives. Managers must have strong interpersonal skills, so they can relate to employees. Communication is one of the most fundamental rules and a quality needed in to be a good manager. They to some degree or another are the coach of the team in the office and they can pick the right people at the proper time to accomplish tasks and delegate to others. A manager is someone who can help employees stay enthused with their job.

Nonprofit Issues and Management

Relationship building is of high importance to the proper operation of the nonprofit. Make sure the office operates properly by holding individual and group meetings. A manager must have good analytical abilities to be able to ascertain the best course of action and set out the necessary strategies. They need to be very logical and consider the thoughts and input of others. Criticism can derail an organization unless it is viewed as constructive. A good manager can distinguish between what is destructive and constructive criticism.

Conflict management is an essential skill for nonprofit managers. They need to be able to acknowledge the feelings of those who are involved to resolve the situation. Generally, it is best to find the main aspects that each person is trying to convey and summarize these points. Find areas of correlation were both parties agree. This way, it is a win-win situation. Instead of a black-and-white picture, where one party goes away disgruntled we need to think in color. Answers are not always easy to find and often require dynamic, colorful thinking. Find areas where both parties can agree and arrive at a consensus. Negotiate an agreement so that parties can conciliate and move on towards the overall objectives.

In this chapter, we have distinguished between the characteristics of a leader and those of a manager. The manager can be a leader and a manager however strictly speaking leadership is a role in and of itself. Ideally the nonprofit organization can have both a person functioning in a leadership role and individual managers of departments who report to the overall leader. Leaders typically are not detail oriented whereas this is a crucial characteristic needed of all managers. Leaders see the big picture while managers can manage the tasks immediately at hand. Both are necessary for the ongoing success of the nonprofit organization. A manager manages people while the leader is typically someone who sets out the overall vision of the organization and assures the directors that the objectives of the organization are being fulfilled. Both roles are crucial for the ongoing success of the nonprofit organization.

Chapter 8. Non-Governmental Organizations

This chapter will show how viable and important non-governmental organization originations and nonprofits are to society. A case will be built to show that because they are so crucial they should not be short changed. Employees in this sector should be paid the same as their counterparts in the for-profit sector. Similarly, their equipment and buildings should be good as well. Reputable, honorable organizations can hold head their heads up high, break a poverty mindset, and work in respectable surrounding. This will help ensure further success when people see themselves as dignified and deserving of proper remuneration.

Non-governmental organizations carry out a crucial role in the relief and development plans of third world countries. There is often mistrust of government leaders and those who operate at arms length can garner greater cooperation from the people. Often too much is expected of the government and realistically speaking the only way people can receive necessary services is if they form cooperatives and other such organizations. Government corporations can become corrupted because of people taking their so-called share. Non-Governmental Organizations need to remember they are not profit-based companies. The private sector can often do a better job than many government agencies because there may be less entanglements. If a corporation wants to succeed it must operate with efficiency and sell a product for which there is a demand. In governments, there is the temptation to just increase taxes to operate, thus building greater resentment.

If people receive money directly from the government they may become dependent upon handouts. However, if a nongovernment organization is providing necessary services there is less dependence on the government. Nongovernmental organizations need to be able to operate regardless of which political party is in power. When government controls and owns everything, it is a communist or socialist form of government. However, when many of the services the public requires are carried out by nongovernmental organizations otherwise know as NGOs there is often greater efficiency.

Greed and corruption can begin to set in when non-governmental organizations and nonprofit organizations forget their mandate. Both nonprofits and NGOs need to continually focus on the initial purpose they were formed to perform. It is easy to become weary in well doing and begin to think one is entitled to a few luxuries. It is at this point that a charitable organization is most vulnerable because salaries can get out of proportion. Salaries are a legitimate overhead expense and often nonprofit organizations do not operate efficiently when they rely too heavily on volunteer help. People are worth what a corresponding job in the for-profit sector would pay. That should be the general rule of thumb to compare salaries in the for-profit and not-for-profit sector. Just because somebody works for charity does not mean they should be paid less than their counterparts.

Often those who work for nonprofit organizations are expected to do more with less. Some leaders think that frugality must always be equated with operating a charity. Granted charities need to cut excess but they should not be expected to operate on shoestring budgets. Often people become exhausted because of a shortage in the workforce. Charities often sell themselves short and work in poor environments without adequate lighting and fresh air. There are no reasons why charitable organizations cannot operate in fresh, bright, modern surroundings. There is often a sense of false humility when carpets are left unclean, desks and chairs broken to try to portray that the charity is frugal. If anything, a large donor coming into a bright modern office will think the leader is successful and worthy of his or her donations. Within reason successful people often have bright modern offices. They are not status symbols however my point is a very simple one; charities need to present themselves as being successful and good at what they do.

There is a foolish notion that charities should operate with broken equipment and second rate facilities. Charities need to view themselves as conducting a very worthwhile service in the community and they are deserving of the finest and best. There are extremes on both sides; frugality that leads to inefficiency and opulence to what is unnecessary. Common sense must prevail always when it comes to expenditures and overhead costs. It is better to spend money up front and get quality equipment and first-rate employees than to suffer setbacks because of buying second-rate equipment and people who will simply take a lower salary.

It is wrong for donors and leaders of nonprofit organizations to expect employees to take a cut in pay and work without the necessary support staff for the so-called good of the nonprofit organization. This leads to disheartenment and resentment in the workforce. Many people are goodhearted and willing to work under difficult circumstances for short-term but overall because of their hard work and efficiency they deserve to be compensated for their labors. The laborer is worthy of his or her pay the same as an ox that can eat grain while it grinds it, the Bible teaches. This poverty mindset and cycle needs to be broken. If leaders of nonprofit organizations and donors see that well compensated employees and proper quality equipment result in greater overall efficiency they will recognize this as a good use of donation or grant money. Again, always balancing this to make sure there are not excesses and opulence that contradict the mission statement.

This is a difficult mindset to break but nonetheless a spiritual stronghold that must be crushed. If companies are profitable and increasing revenues for shareholders, then employees should be rewarded for their efficiency. How much more so in the nonprofit sector when employees put their heart and soul into their work! Fundraisers cannot receive a percentage of the funds they raise. Having said that, if they are effective in raising money their salaries should reflect their level of competency. There is no need to confuse this simple point. What is being said is that businesslike, efficient, educated employees working for a charity have the same rights and deserve the same pay as people in the for-profit sector.

Governments are becoming top-heavy with bureaucracy and nonprofit organizations need to avoid the same entrapment. Increasingly we need non-governmental organizations to conduct public services that have been dumped by the government. The government should govern and leave the care of people in the hands of the people who can do it best. The less government involvement the better when it comes to public services. Government agencies should be operated with the same efficiency as their counterparts in the for-profit sector however that is a discussion for another book. With the high cost of borrowing governments are finding themselves buried in debt because of decades of inefficiency and unrestrained spending. With high taxes and decreased government resources we need the nonprofit sector more than ever to provide care for the public.

We need churches doing more social work instead of less. Much of what the church used to do decades and centuries ago has now been relegated to the government. It is better for the government to funnel money through nongovernmental organizations than to try to do the work itself. We need fewer government social agencies and more independent nonprofit organizations meeting social needs. It is often difficult to balance the workload with the heavy strain of raising funds. However, an effective non-governmental nonprofit organization that is performing a good service in the community should be recognized for their hard work. Hard work, efficiency, and a look of success will help bring in more revenue than otherwise expected.

This mentality that because it is a nonprofit organization it should operate second rate is a terrible fallacy that needs to be overcome. If anything, when it comes to caring for people and carrying out social services a charitable organization or nonprofit should be even better than a for-profit corporation. This is because they have a nobler cause than simply making money and showing a profit at the end of the year. Nonprofit organizations often have noble intentions and have been instituted to carry out very worthwhile causes. If this is the case, then they should be given ample resources and the best equipment and the finest offices to conduct their affairs. If the operators of nonprofit organizations go around with a glum attitude thinking they are not worthy of donations subconsciously this mentality will be conveyed to donors. Rather, if a sense of confidence is conveyed and that the work they are doing is highly important donors will gain confidence knowing their gifts are being used to accomplish noble purposes.

The operators of nonprofit organizations should never think of themselves as second rate employees who could not make it in the for-profit corporation. They should see themselves as highly skilled people who would be recognized as tremendously successful people if they were operating in the for-profit sector. A second-rate mentality produces second rate results. Attention to detail, seeking excellence, and doing one's utmost should be generously rewarded and recognized. People working in the nonprofit sector must take every opportunity they can to gain new skills, certification and even degrees from universities. If the nonprofit sector is set up to care for individual's welfare and other such noble causes the people who receive these services deserve the very finest people from the workforce. Second rate employees flunked out in the for-profit sector should not be working in the nonprofit sector either. If you pay low wages you will not be at able to attract people with the highest aptitude. Rather you will have slovenly people who slack on their job and do second rate work because they are willing to settle for less pay.

An attitude of success and efficiency must mark everything related to a nonprofit organization. In many senses of the word a nonprofit organization should be sharper and better than for-profit corporations. Those who work in for-profit corporations generally are doing so for the money. Those employed by nonprofit organizations are working yes for money but for fine, noble purposes. This can be to the advantage of the leaders of nonprofit organizations because employees put more of their heart into the work. Money is not always a good motivator because you have to keep increasing it to keep people motivated. A sense of purpose will create loyalty on the part of employees when they feel their work is making a difference in the community. Wise leaders of nonprofit organizations would do well to convey regularly the difference their work is making in the lives of appreciative people.

What if in addition to showing pictures of crying, starving children to pull on the heartstrings child aid agencies conveyed financial transparency, gave assurances that moderate amounts were used for administrative/overhead costs and demonstrated donor accountability? They need to be careful to show before and after pictures of children's lives who are improved by donations. Show pictures of the children who are being changed and the ones still in need of help. A simple statement such as, "If money was available to help these other children, we could help them as well," would suffice. I am not trying to be critical of child agencies. I am simply using this as an example. Charities do not need to operate with a sense of devastation and a, "woe is me mentality." They should convey respectability, accountability and transparency. This will help ensure the long-term viability of the nonprofit organization.

Chapter 9. Fund Raising Ideas

Each nonprofit and charity needs to have a brief, introductory letter, describing its formation and purpose. Here is the one I use for the organization I founded. It can serve as an example.

International Harvesters for Christ began over twenty-five years ago when Dr. Jeffrey Lutes travelled as an evangelist to small churches in farming and fishing communities in Atlantic Canada. Today it has a continual evangelistic outreach with radio stations covering major portions of the Maritime Provinces with seven transmitters. During the time this work was developing, ministry opportunities began to open internationally, especially in developing countries. Dr. Lutes began leading crusades and trained nationals in evangelism. Time went on with an overarching concern emerging at home and overseas – care for clergy and their families. International Harvesters for Christ expended substantial resources in support of clergy... from emergency care to nurture and encouragement. Through this, strong and trusting relationships have formed with leaders in various countries.

Harvesters has formed a network of national representatives on four continents who foster service and training within their own country. These include numerous pastors and gospel workers in India, many representatives in Africa and a covert work in a Muslim country. Allow me to present the fourfold focus:

Train and equip leaders in evangelization

Develop strategies to foster national
Kingdom growth

Advance indigenous ministries with special
attention to "closed countries"

Offer two-thirds world leaders an opportunity for education and experience to "walk where Jesus walked" in the Holy Land.

The purpose of this correspondence is to invite you to partner with us to see this project under-girded financially. Our passion is to care for pastors in developing countries. This will be tangible way to demonstrate to them how valuable they are for the eternal kingdom of God.

An introduction must not be wordy and it must explain precisely the purpose of the organization. This will help set the case for support for both donations from individuals and grants from foundations.

Many nonprofit organizations hold an annual appeal. It is a good idea to set a theme for this event and state what the goal is for the project. An appeal can be made for sponsorships from local businesses and individuals. It is wise to have a suggested amount for the organization or individual to give. A business or an individual can be named as a sponsor and have their name on materials and banners that help publicize the event. Send out a letter and give people time to think about the unique opportunity. Increasingly businesses are seeing that it is good for business to be active in the community and giving to worthwhile causes.

It is very important to have a monthly newsletter going forth. There is great emphasis on social media however at the end of the day regular mail still proves to be one of the most effective ways to raise money for a nonprofit. State a problem to be solved and show the potential donor how they can be part of the solution. Here is an example; poor people in developing countries often do not have access to clean water and the result is needless disease and even death. Show people how a simple filter can help remove contaminants and allow people to have healthy families. Their donation can make a tremendous difference in the life of a family. People feel like they are part of the solution when fundraising is presented this way.

Nonprofit Issues and Management

It is extremely important when people give they are thanked for their donation. A person should receive a thank you note within two weeks. It makes a tremendous difference when people are acknowledged for their gift. For people giving larger gifts it may be appropriate to send a fruit basket or a book as a way of saying thank you. Every gift should be followed up with a thank you and a receipt. If this is done promptly and efficiently people are likely to give again.

The charitable organization needs to show accountability by providing financial reports. Graphs showing how the money is being utilized are effective. When people feel appreciated and there is a sense of transparency on the part of the organization they are likely to give a second or third time. People have a right to know how their gift is being used and the difference it is making. When possible provide the operating budget, and give specific examples of how the money is being used.

It is extremely important to have a donation page that is easily navigated. It needs to be seen on a handheld device easily as well because many people will begin utilizing their mobile phone to donate. The page should be very clear and not have a lot of superfluities. It basically should be a one-two three-step process making it as easy as possible to give online. There should always be somebody available to answer the telephone because many people want to give over the phone instead of on line

It is important to work closely with a financial planner so that you can encourage people to include your charity in their estate planning. A knowledgeable financial planner can help family members to see that it is a win-win situation for the inheritors and charity. The donation receipt will help offset some of the tax. Rather than the charity being left out altogether it is possible to include the charity in the will and the tax receipt help offset money that otherwise would end up going to the government.

Some people may consider making a financial investment on the part of the charity and allowing the nonprofit organization to receive the interest. The person continues to hold the principal or the give the investment directly to the charity to manage. This is a way for the gift to have an ongoing effect. The donor may choose to hold onto the initial gift in case they need the money at a future time and give on an annual basis the amount earned by the investment.

It is possible to name the charity as the holder of a life insurance policy with the donor giving the premiums. The monthly amount can be receipted in part. This is especially important for charities that are reliant on elderly donors. This way when the senior donors pass away the charity continues to function strongly. It is a way for the donor to leave a legacy for their favorite charity.

A simple, one page monthly letter sent in the mail should not be overlooked. Seniors make up a sizable percentage of the donors to most charities. Many of them issue checks and having a self-addressed envelope makes it easier for them to give. The letter should tell a story of someone's life that has been changed through the charity. Present a problem and how the donor can be part of the solution. There should be a lot of white space on the letter. In other words, it should not be verbose. A letter should be sent eleven times a year to keep the charity in the minds of the donors.

People appreciate personal contact from the charity. Build strong relationships with those who give. Establish trust and a sense of accountability. Remembering people at their birthdays is thoughtful. Sending a book that has special note in the front is meaningful. When possible set up a booth at conferences to meet potential and existing donors in person. Use things such as pens, letter openers and other practical gifts with the name of the mission on it to keep the organization before the people.

Facebook advertising is effective because you can target your audience. For example, you can select a 100-kilometer radius around a certain city and use keywords such as Bible, Christian, church etc. if it is a Christian organization. Monthly emails are important to keep the constitutes in touch with the organization. Fund raising dinners with a special is helpful too. Radio, television and magazine advertising is helpful when the organization can incorporate the costs into its budget.

I am not an advocate of expecting that a professional fund raising firm is going to be the magic bullet to tremendously increase donations. The best foundations to approach for grants are the ones where there is a relationship with the directors and they have come to value the work of the organization. Generally, if the organization wants to grow its funding base it is best to look to those who have given significant gidfts in the pass and realizing it is quite possible for example if they have given thousands they may give tens of thousands. The only reason is because they haven't been asked. In conclusion there is no substitute for building a slow, steady relationship with donors.

Chapter 10. Encouragement

Those operating a nonprofit organization need to be able to build themselves up when they feel torn down. We can encourage ourselves when we identify our feelings and take positive action. Often you must encourage yourself because there may be no one else to do it for you. There are many things to discourage people in nonprofit organizations. It could be someone in the organization who is critical of your leadership, your ideas or even you as a person. We need to learn how to overcome opposition, difficulty and criticism.

There can be very discouraging situations, such as people wanting you to resign. Employees can turn against you. Finances could be low and you need to encourage yourself." The theme of this chapter is how to overcome discouragement and keep on going on when everything seems bleak. The main point that I want to emphasize is we must encourage ourselves to overcome discouragement, self-doubt and opposition.

Step one - Be determined to persevere. – Improvise

Step two - Take control of your feelings. – Rationalize

Step three - Objectify see the whole picture - Organize

Step four – Formulate a strategy - Standardize

Step five - Do not succumb to defeat despair - Mobilize

Step six – Give yourself to meditation - Utilize

Step seven - Give yourself proper rest - Normalize

Step eight - Look for the hand of God - Formalize

When we are tired and anxious we may find, ourselves doing strange things. When we are stressed we can be vulnerable and susceptible to attack. My advice to you is to engage in personal renewal. We all go through seasons in our lives of fatigue and discouragement. Do what you must to survive. Don't allow the criticisms and gossip of others prevent you from you being effective. Overcome discouragement by seeking advice from wise people and encourage yourself. Tough times do not last. Tough people do.

You may have people who are subverting your leadership and possibly even trying to get you dismissed from employment. Look for an ally if this is the case. This person may be basically your only friend but none the less they can help you to fight to hold your place. Some people want to bring retaliation for a salary cut. Dismissal of an employee and retaliation by friend may be one among any number of reasons for going through a tough time at work. My advice is to size up the situation, overcome, encourage yourself and maintain your leadership.

Life can have some strange twists and turns. We need to be prepared for the unexpected. Attempts to have you dismissed from your job can be about one of worse things that could ever happen to a person. It is a serious thing to lose your job but whatever you do protect your family. Sometimes circumstances are beyond our control and there's nothing you can do about it. This can be one of the lowest points in your life. Here is a poem that has brought me comfort over the years:

Don't Quit

When things go wrong, as they sometimes will,

when the road you're trudging seems all uphill,

When the funds are low and the debts are high,

And you want to smile, but you have to sigh,

When care is pressing you down a bit,

Rest, if you must, but do not quit.

Life is queer with its twists and turns,

As every one of us sometimes learns,

And many a failure turns about,

When he might have won had he stuck it out;

Don't give up though the pace seems slow

You may succeed with another blow.

Often the goal is nearer than,

It seems to a faint and faltering man,

Often the struggler has given up,

When he might have captured the victors cup,

And he learned too late when the night slipped down,

How close he was to the golden crown.

Nonprofit Issues and Management

Success is failure turned inside out

The silver tint of the clouds of doubt,

And you never can tell how close you are,

It may be near when it seems so far,

So, stick to the fight when you're hardest hit

Its when things seem worst that you must not quit.

These are some of the name put forward as the author of the poem: Edgar A Guest, Larry S. Chengges, Rick Frutell, Leo Padgett , Joe David Harrison, Sam Candelaria, Clinton Howell, Frank Collins and Gerard Haughey. The US Copyright Office recognizes the poem as public domain.

Have you ever cried heaves and sobs until you were exhausted? Be in touch with your feelings however do not leave it there. Put your emotions at the end of the train and don't allow them to be the engine. Manage your emotions and do not allow them to dictate to you. This is a step-in overcoming depression. Take control of your feelings. Generally, an action can reverse or align your emotions into proper balance. Do not stay in the depths of despair. Be determined to persevere. – Improvise and take control of your feelings. Then it is important to rationalize. Be determined to persevere and take control of your feelings.

In our electronic age, it appears that technology while yes saves us labor, it increases our stress. We can be so overwhelmed with tasks, being constantly accessible to people, and helping so many others with their difficulties that we become burned out. We need to refuel ourselves, take time for proper rest and be certain that we do not allow ourselves to become depleted spiritually.

Encourage yourself by positive affirmation. It is good to look to a friend and even a counselor to help us in times of depression. However, there may come a point when we cannot look to other people. We must encourage ourselves. We need to give ourselves positive, self-talk and rely on the promises of God's Bible to pull ourselves through. This takes will and self-determination. If we give up, then we stay defeated.

We need to realize that we are not just fighting against individuals but sometimes mindsets. Don't allow yourself to wallow in depression. Do not accept circumstances, instead of fighting against them. Sometimes all you can do is to just stand your ground. Most of what we worry about never comes to pass. Worry deprives us of the mental energy to focus on developing a solution. Overcome the battle for the mind. Do not allow yourself to be tormented with negative, self-deprecating thoughts.

Often great leaders go through difficult circumstances. Abraham Lincoln faced a civil war. Winston Churchill had been defeated politically yet when the war broke out his country wanted him back. Just as there are physically strong people so too are there people who are emotionally strong. If we want to be strong in the natural realm we exercise. If we want to be strong emotionally then we need to exercise ourselves emotionally. Sometimes it takes hard work. We need to be emotionally healthy and strong. An emotionally healthy person can think through discouraging circumstances and be encouraged.

Sometimes we just may become so weary that we must take a rest. Remember the poem that we shared earlier. It is all right to take a rest so long as we do not quit in our work. In overcoming depression, it is important to give ourselves the rest we need. We need to be honest with ourselves and admit our weaknesses. This may entail a brief time away from work to gain a new perspective.

Look for God's hand to be at work in your circumstances when you are faced with difficulty. Be assured that He has not abandoned you and that He will meet you at your point of need. We can rest assured that God will be with us in our trials as well. Spirituality can help us to overcome depression and find resilience to face challenges in the work place.

What we learned is take a rest and whatever you do don't quit. There is another principle that we have learned, as well. You cannot always expect that others are going to encourage you. You will often have to do this for yourself. You may find yourself in very difficult circumstances. Do not give up and do whatever it takes to keep yourself refreshed and encouraged.

There are different meanings for heat. When we refer to heat that is produced by a stove or from the sun we are referencing what is measured in Celsius. The heat we're talking about in this chapter is a proverbial one. Pressure or stress are not as easily measured but every bit as real. Our objective today is to learn how to stand up under difficulties and overcome opposition. Our goal is to become less bothered by trials and be better prepared to overcome them when they arise.

We all face heat in one form or another. It may be from an employer who is insisting on us meeting a deadline. It could be a spouse who is very demanding or a child who struggles in school. Deadlines, threats of physical violence, family pressures; these are just some of the types of heat we face figuratively. We need to learn how to stay cool when we're under pressure. You may be facing tensions in the home, and tensions in the office at the same time. If so, govern your thoughts because this is the way to subdue anxiety and fear.

Our theme is that you can prepare for tense situations and rise to overcome them with confidence. What do you do when people have grave misgivings about you? While we cannot control the circumstances on the outside, we can certainly have peace on the inside. Prayer, reflection, quiet contemplation, meditation and intercession will create a thermal barrier so to speak to help you endure the heat of life's trials and struggles.

We are to do our best to bring reconciliation with disgruntled people. Sadly, however this is not always possible. To have calm minds we simply must accept this as a fact; not everyone is going to seek reconciliation. Some are purposely vindictive. Not everyone has malicious intent, though. If it is possible we should seek to be at peace with one another. If we can't, then we simply must move on.

We are often intimidated by what other people think. One of the best ways to defeat worry and anxiety in our lives is to prepare in advance. When you are facing, a trial think of what the questions will be and prepare in advance in your mind what your response to the attacks will be that you face. This will help to counteract worry. When you are under verbal attack remember to be humble and do not take it personally. If our character is being called into question we do not need to be defensive. This will help us to stay cool when the heat is on.

By times we can feel unrealistic expectations are being placed on us. Some may want to push us into a role that is not designed for us. You may feel the heat is on when you are pushed into a job that you don't feel qualified to accomplish. Don't allow people to pressure you into something not designed for you. Simply be who God created you to be. This will turn the temperature down, symbolically speaking. One of the best ways to stand up under pressure is to stay focused on what your purpose is meant to be. Do not allow others to squeeze you into their mold. When you feel that people are putting unrealistic expectations on you don't succumb to the pressure to conform to what they want you to be. Stay true to your calling

Who among us does not need encouragement from time to time? Remember this sentence that I am about to declare to you when you are tempted to despair. Never give up when you are engaged in a faithful cause. We all face hardship in this life. Remain strong as you face hardships. A thought running throughout all that I have said to you is, you can confidently face and overcome difficulties.

You may be facing people who are insolent and disrespectful to you. Stay true to what compelled you to enter this field in the first place. Stay on course despite the insults hurled at you. Stand strong in the face of hardship. We may set out with noble intentions but it is not long before we run into hardship. "Do not become weary in well doing, for in due season we shall reap if we faint not," (Gal. 6:9). It is easy to become fearful and lose heart when we face opposition. Here is a poem about perseverance,

When all the world is looming dark

And things seem not so clear,

When shadows seem to hover 'round Lord,

may I persevere.

When it seems everything's been tried

And there's no way to go,

Just let me keep remembering

Sometimes the journey's slow.

I may just need to stop and rest

Along the path I trod,

A time to try to understand

And have my talk with God.

As I gain new strength to carry on

Without a doubt or fear,

Somehow I know things will be right,

And so, I persevere.

By Anne Stortz

Here are some quotes to encourage you today. "Our greatest weakness lies in giving up. The most certain way to succeed is always to try just one more time" Thomas Alva Edison - inventor (1847-1931). "Most of the important things in the world have been accomplished by people who have kept on trying when there seemed to be no help at all" Dale Carnegie – writer (1888-1955). "Remember to show permanence, perseverance and persistence despite all obstacles, discouragements, and impossibilities: It is this, that in all things distinguishes the strong soul from the weak" Thomas Carlyle (1795-1881) British historian and essayist.

When faced with hardship, we may be tempted to use dishonest means to try to solve our problems. Some people cheat because they think they deserve a break in life. Adhere to your principles and have faith, that in the end everything will work out for your good.

Situation ethics is a Christian ethical theory that was developed in the 1960s by an Episcopal priest named Joseph Fletcher. It basically states that sometimes moral principles can be cast aside in certain situations if love is best served. Truth is not subjective like love often is in our thinking. We need to have moral absolutes and we need to stay true to ourselves when we face the heat. When you are faced with hardships and difficulties do not compromise your moral principles as a way of escape no matter what the situation. Honesty is its own reward. Wrong is wrong if everyone says it is right. Right is right even if everyone says it is wrong. Stay on course if even you must do it alone.

Think of the ramifications of giving up. Many people depend upon you. There is a great temptation when we are persecuted and under attack to pull back and hide our light. We must not succumb to this allurement to quit. We need to be faithful to our mandate. Even if you experience delays in life and great disappointments do not become bitter and resentful. However, in the face of disappointments and hardships we must remain firm in our resolve. Stay in the place where you are called to work. You will know when it is time to leave your post.

You can expect that people will lie about you and try to distort your reputation. By times it will feel like we are going to crack under the pressure. We will experience prolonged periods of testing. The main point that I want to convey is do not become discouraged and give up in your ministry. Persevere! You will see one day that it has been worth it.

Conclusion

We learned the importance of developing a mission statement to serve as a guiding principle for everything the organization that's. We also recognize the importance of ethical practices when it comes to money so that the organization continues to operate properly. While there are differences and similarities between nonprofits and for-profits nonprofit organizations have unique qualities. There are obstacles that face nonprofit organizations today however with. strategies they can continue to operate reliably. It will be a test of mettle for the leader to be able to keep the nonprofit operating properly. There are going to be many personnel problems however with proper skills the leader can overcome them. It is important for the leader to remain encouraged in the face of so many obstacles and difficulties.

A mission statement is like a compass to keep the nonprofit going in the right direction. For example, Google's mission is to organize the world's information and make it universally accessible and useful. Disney states, "We create happiness by providing the finest entertainment for people of all ages." These brief and powerful statements set out the direction for the organizations they represent. We looked at the mission statements for a variety of companies and organizations and determined to be effective one needs to have a clearly stated purpose. It keeps the organization moving straight ahead and dispensing with what is unnecessary or a detraction.

This book looked at how important image and the importance of maintain good relations with donors. Gimmicks never pay off in the long run. Only what is ethical and totally above board should be implemented by a nonprofit organization. A sense of accountability needs to be upheld always. These standards will help to ensure long term viability.

A great deal of time was spent comparing nonprofit to for-profit corporations. The point was clearly demonstrated that in no way should nonprofits be second rate and operating with lower standards. Similar to for-profits nonprofits need to keep an eye on their fiscal house. Ideals must not be allowed to overshadow practicality as is sometimes the case with nonprofit organizations. There are great rewards for those who work in nonprofit organizations because they're doing things like helping humanity regardless of the economic benefit. Wnefit. We also emphasized that nonprofit organizations need to embrace innovative ideas and approaches for carrying out their mandate. They need to be willing to change and adapt to their surroundings. Nonprofit organizations should be among the most efficiently operated and effective organizations that exist.

Nonprofit organizations may start off with lofty ideals but soon run amok because adequate preparations were not taken. We discussed the long-term viability of nonprofits that can occur with new strategies and the implementation of clever ideas. Creativity needs be welcomed at all time. Technology is constantly changing and nonprofit organizations need to keep on top of these changes. Strategic planning needs to take place to establish priorities. The nonprofit organization that embraces innovative ideas and has an unobstructed vision for the future is one that will remain viable and sustainable

It can be very difficult to operate nonprofit particularly during an economic downturn. However, the public realizes that one of the first places to be affected is the nonprofit sector. Nonprofits need to work especially well during difficult financial times. During a downturn when money is scarce nonprofits can still succeed if they present matters properly. When financial conditions are poor there is a temptation to put a freeze on hiring and not allow for salary increases. Those who operate nonprofit organizations need to be reminded that their employees should be remunerated properly. While being frugal is important it is also important to implement effective strategies. Nonprofit organizations need to work harder than ever to present a case for donations. If potential donors feel their donations are being used responsibly and a nonprofit organization is working hard to carry out their objectives they may continue to give when money scarce.

Nonprofit organizations face many of the same problems as for-profit Corporation. They are not exempt from personnel problems and certain measures need be implemented to be certain there is high performance on the part of employees. Every organization needs to have periodic performance evaluations for employees. This provides an opportunity for feedback both from the employer and from the employees to the employer. Information needs to be clearly delineated in the employee handbook. There should be nothing second-rate about nonprofit organizations. If anything, there should be higher standards for nonprofit organizations.

Nonprofit organizations need to have effective managers. an effective manager is one who is a good listener and communicates well with the employees. A nonprofit manager needs to be positive and optimistic without being overconfident. Negativity and needs to be addressed immediately to keep a positive atmosphere. The nonprofit manager will set a good example. Employees need to be inspired and motivated in order for the nonprofit organization to function well. It is the role of the manager to create a good dynamic within the organization. The manager must build strong relationships with the employees and take seriously the task of conflict management.

The obstacles facing nonprofit organizations can be daunting. However, the manager can stay optimistic and effective. It is my hope that this book has provided keen insight to encourage managers of nonprofit organizations. The more a manager knows the better equipped they are to handle and overcome. It is a high and noble calling to serve a nonprofit organization. There are ideals in a nonprofit that are not typical of for-profit corporations. Stay encouraged and be the best you can be.

www.ingramcontent.com/pod-product-compliance
Lightning Source LLC
Chambersburg PA
CBHW071439180526
45170CB00001B/381